World Religions & Cults 101

Bruce BICKEL
&
Stan JANTZ

HARVEST HOUSE PUBLISHERS
EUGENE, OREGON

CHRISTIANITY 101 is a registered trademark of Bruce Bickel and Stan Jantz. Harvest House Publishers, Inc., is the exclusive licensee of the federally registered trademark CHRISTIANITY 101.

Cover by Left Coast Design, Portland, Oregon

Cover illustration © Krieg Barrie Illustration

WORLD RELIGIONS AND CULTS 101
Formerly titled *Bruce & Stan's® Guide to Cults, Religions, and Spiritual Beliefs*
Copyright © 2002 by Bruce Bickel and Stan Jantz
Published by Harvest House Publishers
Eugene, Oregon 97402
www.harvesthousepublishers.com

Library of Congress Cataloging-in-Publication Data

Bickel, Bruce, 1952–
        [Bruce & Stan's guide to cults, religions, spiritual beliefs]
        World religions and cults 101 / Bruce Bickel and Stan Jantz.
                p.cm.—(Christianity 101)
        Includes bibliographical references and index.

        ISBN-13: 978-0-7369-1263-1

        1. Religions. 2. Cults. I. Title: World religions and cults one hundred one. II. Title: World religions and cults one hundred and one. III. Jantz, Stan, 1952– IV. Title. V. Series.
        BL80.3.B53 2005
        200—dc22

                                                                              2004020038

Printed in the United States of America

Contents

About the Authors

Bruce Bickel is an attorney who specializes in estate planning and trust law. He is also a corporate motivational speaker whose ministry involvements include preaching and speaking at Christian conferences.

Stan Jantz managed a chain of Christian retail stores for more than 25 years. Currently he is a marketing consultant and a partner in a community-building software company.

Together Bruce and Stan have written more than 50 books with more than 2½ million copies sold.

About Our Adviser

Dr. Craig Hazen, associate professor of comparative religion and Christian apologetics at Biola University, is the adviser for *World Religions and Cults 101*. Throughout this book you will find Dr. Hazen's comments and insights, which are marked with the heading, "Dr. Hazen Adds..." He received his Ph.D. in religious studies from the University of California at Santa Barbara. As the founder and director of the Master of Arts program in Christian apologetics at Biola, Dr. Hazen has lectured worldwide on the historical reliability of Scripture, religion and science, and Christianity among world religions. He is the author of numerous articles and books, and is the editor of the scholarly journal *Philosophia Christi*.

A Note from the Authors

*L*et's get it out in the open, right up front. We are fully devoted followers of Jesus Christ. In the spectrum of world religions and spiritual beliefs, that puts us smack-dab in the middle of Christianity. There. Now we said it. No one can accuse us of pretending to be objective while surreptitiously concealing an innate bias.

Perhaps you are a reader who has a different spiritual point of view (or none at all yet). If so, you might be worried that our prejudice will affect our objectivity. We don't blame you for being worried at the outset. But let us assure you that while your opinions may differ, our purposes are aligned with yours:

- You don't want to read a one-sided, intolerant, discriminatory tirade against other faiths. And we don't want to write a book like that.

- You are interested in an impartial, unbiased explanation of various religious viewpoints. So are we.

Is it possible for two guys who strongly believe in one faith to write objectively about other religions? We think so, and we have done our absolute best to maintain our neutrality so you can evaluate the various religions for yourself. (Hey, Bruce is a lawyer, so his career is all about presenting the good points of a case he doesn't necessarily believe in. And Stan's background is in retail marketing, so he knows the benefits of comparative shopping.)

But rather than trying to impress you with our efforts to maintain a neutral perspective, perhaps you will be most relieved if we just tell you why we wrote this book. Here is our purpose, plain and simple: to provide an understandable overview of predominant religions and spiritual beliefs (with a little sense of humor thrown in along the way). That's it. We are not attempting to convert, cajole, or coax you into Christianity. Yes, we think that you ought to give the spiritual dimension of your life serious consideration. But no, we don't want to force or trick you into what we believe. We are proponents of information, but we oppose indoctrination. The choices you make ought to be your own.

We might get a little flak from the Christian community for suggesting that you consider other religions along with Christianity. (It won't be the first time we have invited a little criticism upon ourselves.) But there are already too many books that try to force a certain religion on you. This isn't going to be another one of them.

If your purpose in reading this book is to find a faith of your own, that's great. We're glad that we could help you get started. But don't stop here. Use this book as a springboard to further investigation and analysis. Our goal is to get you thinking about spiritual matters. We hope we accomplish that.

Introduction

*W*hat's *A*head

Every single person thinks about God. Now, he or she may picture God as—

- an impersonal force that infuses every part of the universe, or
- a spirit that inhabits every person like a kind of divine light, or
- a powerful Creator who made the universe and then took a long vacation, never to return, or
- a personal spirit being who made the universe and then stayed very involved, or
- something that doesn't exist at all.

But in one way or another everyone has a God idea. We don't know you very well (yet), but we suspect that you probably fall somewhere into one of those categories. It's also likely that when God comes to your thoughts,

- you already know what you believe, but you would like to know more; or
- you aren't really sure if your belief in God is the right one, but it's working, so you're going to stick with what you believe (for now); or

- you are open to beliefs about God other than your own because you've been told that one God idea is as good as another; or

- you are very sure you have the right belief, but you would like to know more about what other people believe so you can relate to them.

Notice that each of these "God idea" descriptions contain the word *believe* or *belief*. There's a reason for that. All people accept the fact that *something* is true or real, even if they aren't sure what that something is. That's what belief is. So far that sounds pretty ordinary, but believe us, belief can get pretty exciting because it goes to the heart of who you are. As a human being, you don't just believe in the obvious, such as your own existence. You think on a much higher level. You want to know...

- Why are you here?
- How did you get here?
- How do you fit into the world?
- When your life is over, where do you go?

That's what belief is all about—answering these questions about life and what it means. Somewhere in the process of finding the answers to these questions, most people hope they will find some kind of ultimate reality, otherwise known as God. And that's why religions exist in the first place. They are human attempts to sort out and answer those questions every person asks, and then to put the answers into some sort of belief system.

What This Book Is All About

This is a book about the world's most important cults, religions, and spiritual beliefs.

Since four-fifths of the people living on earth today practice some kind of religion, we figure there is a pretty good market for a book like this. Of course, we're just two ordinary guys from California, so you may wonder how our book is going to relate to someone practicing Zen Buddhism in the Himalayan foothills. Not to worry! We don't have to relate to the Buddhist in China. We've got plenty of Buddhists right here in our home state, along with a number of Hindus and Muslims and people who practice hundreds of other religions and belief systems.

The Religious Population of the World*
(In thousands)

Christians (total)	1,955,229
Roman Catholics	981,465
Protestants	404,020
Orthodox	218,350
Anglicans	69,136
Other Christians	282,258
Muslims	1,126,325
Nonreligious	886,929
Hindus	793,076
Buddhists	325,275
Atheists	222,195
Chinese Folk Religionists	220,971
New Religionists	106,016
Ethnic Religions	102,945
Sikhs	19,508
Jews	13,866
Spiritists	10,293
Baha'is	6,404
Confucians	5,086
Jains	4,920
Shintoists	2,898
Other Religionists	1,952

(handwritten annotations: "23.2 B", "Increase by", "73%", "Indian" next to Sikhs, "Indian" next to Baha'is)

* The *Time Almanac 2000*, Borgna Brunner, ed. (Des Moines, IA: Time Inc., 2000), p. 404.

You see, Buddhists, Hindus, and Muslims (and all their derivatives) no longer live exclusively in the "foreign fields." America
is the most religiously diverse nation in the world, and chances
are your own neighborhood has its share of people who believe
much differently than you do, but with just as much sincerity and
devotion.

With that in mind, we didn't write this book to simply catalog
and describe the religions "out there," like we might tell you about
the planets in our solar system (you know they exist, but you're
never going to visit them). Unlike the planets, the religions of the
world have come to your door, and we want to help you sort
through and understand what they teach and what their followers
believe. That's what this book is all about.

Dr. Hazen Adds...

*T*he intense human drive to find meaning in life, to worship something, to cover guilt, and to seek guidance from above is such a universal and enduring trait of human beings that some scholars of religion
think that the species name for humans should be Homo religious (the
religious man) rather than Homo sapiens (the wise man).

Why You Need to Read This Book

There's a common belief out there that all religions basically
contain the same truth, only they present it in different ways. It's
the "God by any other name is still God" concept (with apologies
to William Shakespeare). According to this view, God lives at the
top of a very big mountain, and all the religions and belief systems in the world are like different trails that make their way to
the top. Just like every trail eventually reaches the summit, every
religion eventually reaches God.

There's only one problem with this thinking: *All religions can't
be true.* How can we be so sure? Because all religions are different
and mutually exclusive at various points, as we're going to discover
together in this book. Rather than say all religions are true, it would
be more reasonable to believe they are all false, or that only one
of them is true and the others are false.

At this point you may be wondering, "Doesn't every religion contain at least *some* truth?" Absolutely. But that doesn't mean the entire religion is true. As we are fond of saying:

There is truth in everything, but not everything is true.

When it comes to God and your eternal destiny (a pretty important part of any religion, by the way), doesn't it make sense to make sure your beliefs are as true as they can be? After all, this is your life we're talking about here. That's why we will do our best to help you sort out the truth by comparing the world's major belief systems.

In part 1 we're going to look at the three main monotheistic religions: Christianity, Judaism, and Islam. These are the religions that believe in one true God.

In part 2 we'll consider some blended belief systems, often referred to as cults. These belief systems have elements of monotheism, but some of them also feature *polytheism* (that is, many gods).

Part 3 includes the philosophical religions, which can be best described by the term *pantheistic monism,* meaning they see all things as God, and all things as one.

The belief systems built on the premise that God is who or what you want Him to be—or totally unnecessary, or even nonexistent—make up part 4. These spiritual beliefs are best characterized by the terms *syncretism* and *naturalism.*

Finally, in part 5 we'll try to help you come to some conclusions about your own beliefs.

This Book Is for You If . . .

Maybe you aren't exactly struggling with your own beliefs, but you're feeling like you need to know more about what other people believe. Or perhaps you aren't as confident in what you believe and you want to know how it stacks up with the beliefs of other people. Either way, we think this book will meet your needs if...

- You know what you believe, but you want to know why it's true.

- You are confident that you have chosen the one true belief system, but you want to better understand the things that make it true.

- You want to become more aware of the major differences between your beliefs and the beliefs of other people.

- You believe that there is some truth in other religions, and you want to know what it is so you can better understand the people who follow these religions.

- You want to learn about other religions because you desire to share your faith.

A Few More Comments Before You Begin

Already you have probably noticed that this book is rather unconventional. We have been called "self-proclaimed nonexperts," and it's a description we gladly accept. We're on the same journey you are, only we've had a chance to study ahead a little bit and regurgitate the information in a more user-friendly style than you're likely to find in scholarly textbooks. But we wanted to make sure we are giving you the straight scoop, so we asked a brilliant professor of comparative religions to review our manuscript. Dr. Craig Hazen was kind enough to give our book a good going-over, and we've included his comments throughout the book.

We would like very much for this to be an interactive book, but that depends on you! If you have any comments or questions, please contact us. Tell us what you think about the book, ask a question, or share an experience of your own. We want to hear from you, and we promise to respond. You can contact us at:

E-mail: info@christianity101online.com
Website: www.christianity101online.com
Snail mail: c/o Twelve Two Media, P.O. Box 25997,
             Fresno, CA 93729

At www.christianity101online.com, you'll find more resources and additional questions. You can also ask your own questions, and you can find answers to some of the most frequently asked questions about world religions and cults.

Now that we're done with preliminaries and introductions, let's get to the topic at hand. Let's learn about the world's religions and cults.

Part I
One-God Religions

Chapter 1

> I believe in Christianity as I believe that the sun has risen, not only because I see it, but because by it I see everything else.
>
> *C.S. Lewis*

A lot of people are calling themselves Christians these days—nearly two billion people, to be exact. Eighty-six percent of self-professing Christians are either Roman Catholic (50 percent), Protestants (21 percent), Orthodox (11 percent), or Anglican (4 percent). That leaves 14 percent—or nearly 300 million people—who call themselves Christians but aren't necessarily affiliated with a traditional church or group.

So how do you sort it all out? How do you finally define *Christian* and *Christianity?* One way is to modify the name *Christian* with the adjective *biblical*. That is to say, biblical Christianity takes its truth from the Bible as God's eternal Word.

Another term Christians sometimes use to further designate their beliefs is *Christ-follower*, because ultimately a biblical Christian follows the belief system named for its founder, Jesus Christ. That seems appropriate because, at its heart, Christianity is all about belief in Jesus.

Christianity:
All About Jesus

$\mathcal{W}$hat's $\mathcal{A}$head

- ☐ Why Start with Christianity?
- ☐ God: You Can Take Him at His Word
- ☐ Jesus: The Answer to Our Problem
- ☐ Church: Why Bother?

*C*hristianity has a lot in common with many of the other religions we're going to talk about in this book. Christianity features just one God, but so do Judaism and Islam. Christianity emphasizes the importance of relationships and the family, just like Mormonism. The Christian Bible talks about meditating. That sounds like Hinduism.

So what sets Christianity apart from all the other religions of the world? That's an easy answer. In fact, we can answer it in just one word: *Jesus*. Christianity may have some things in common with other religions, but there's one huge difference. Other religions may acknowledge that Jesus was a great teacher, a prophet, or one of many sons of God. But only Christianity holds Jesus up as *the* Son of God, equal to God in every way, who came to earth to save sinners and to give them eternal life.

Not only is Jesus the cornerstone of Christianity, but the person of Jesus Christ—His life, death, and resurrection—is also the centerpiece of human history. In the 2000 years since Jesus walked the earth, no other person has had such an impact on the world. Nearly one-third of the six billion people living on the planet right now claim to follow the religion that bears His name. In this way Christianity is more than a religious system or a way of life. Christianity is all about a personal God who loved humanity so much that He sent His only Son, Jesus, to show us the way.

Why Start with Christianity?

As we begin this book on world religions and cults, you might be wondering if it's appropriate to start with Christianity. Aren't we being a little prejudiced, given our personal beliefs? Shouldn't we present all of the other religions before we get to Christianity so that you can make an objective evaluation without being influenced by our own bias?

We thought about doing it that way, but then Dr. Craig Hazen, our adviser for this book, convinced us to start with Christianity rather than finish with it. "It's the only religion that's testable," he said. "So you need to start with Christianity and measure all of the other religions against it rather than the other way around." Dr. Hazen explained that this feature of Christianity is unnerving to many because people generally conclude that religion is subjective. They think it's merely a personal experience that takes place inside you. What you believe really doesn't matter as long as you're sincere.

Well, that's fine if you're talking about the flavor of your favorite ice cream or the color of your socks. Your personal preference with regard to taste or fashion doesn't have a big effect on your future. But when it comes to your life and where you're going to spend eternity, what you believe needs to be rooted in objective truth rather than subjective opinion. How else will you know for sure that you believe the right thing? Dr. Hazen believes—and we agree—that Christianity is the one religion that can be tested objectively and found to be true.

Does this mean that all the other religions are entirely false? Not at all. As we said in the introduction, every religion contains some truth, but not every religion is true, and by that we mean *completely* true. The one exception is Christianity, which claims to be completely true because...

*T*rue spirituality cannot be abstracted from truth at one end, nor from the whole man and the whole culture at the other. If there is a true spirituality, it must encompass all. The Bible insists that truth is one—and it is almost the sole surviving system in our generation that does.

Francis Schaeffer

1. Christianity is completely true in what it says about God.
All religions and belief systems talk about God and the supernatural world in one way or another, but only Christianity presents God as He really is: the self-existent, eternal, personal Creator God who has revealed Himself to humankind. Why do we believe this is the true picture of God? Because that's what God has said about Himself. It's true because we can take God at His Word, as we will discover shortly.

2. Christianity is completely true to the way things really are.
What we mean by this is that Christianity gives reasonable explanations for the way things are in the natural world. First, the truths of Christianity are consistent with *history*. The Bible is filled with facts about real people and real events in real time in ways that can be verified. Second, the truths of Christianity are consistent with *science*. The Bible is not a scientific book, but the explanations it gives for how the universe got here are compatible with what science tells us is true. Finally, the truths of Christianity are consistent with *reason*. This means that rational beings (such as you) can objectively evaluate the Christian belief system and find that it is reasonable and noncontradictory in its approach to the human condition. The philosopher Francis Schaeffer wrote:

> This does not mean that the Christian answer should be accepted for pragmatic reasons, but it does mean that the solution given in the Bible answers the problem of the universe and man, and nothing else does.

With that in mind, let's look a little closer at the God of Christianity, the person of Jesus, and the church founded in His name.

A Quick Look at Christianity

- Christianity is a religion based on the life and teachings of Jesus Christ.

- Following the death, resurrection, and ascension of Jesus in A.D. 30 in Jerusalem, the message of Jesus was carried throughout the known world by the disciples of Jesus, also called apostles.

- Because the first converts to this new belief system were Jews, Christianity was first viewed as a sect of Judaism.

- Gradually the new believers, instructed and encouraged by the apostle Paul, saw their faith as distinct from Judaism.

- The followers of Jesus were first called Christians in Antioch, Syria (present-day Turkey).

- The Romans destroyed Jerusalem in A.D. 70, effectively scattering Jews and Christians alike.

- Over the centuries Christianity has developed along three main lines: Eastern Orthodoxy, Roman Catholicism, and Protestantism.

- Today approximately 1.9 billion people practice some form of Christianity within these three groups.

God: You Can Take Him at His Word

The most powerful and pervasive idea in the world is the idea of God. Every person who has ever lived has thought about God (even the people who deny God exists think about Him). Yet God is more than an idea we humans came up with. God is a very real spirit Being who has always existed and will forever exist.

God Is Real

Different religions describe God as a force, a universal principle, or a superhuman cosmic grandfather who sits on a white throne somewhere, disengaged from His lowly subjects. This is not the God of biblical Christianity. The God of the Bible is real. He has a personality with real characteristics:

- **God is self-existent.** Everything that exists has a cause, and the first cause of everything is God, who Himself has no cause. This is not double-talk or a contradiction in terms. Logic and reason dictate that for anything to exist, there must first be an uncaused, self-existent being. The Bible says, "In the beginning God created the heavens and the earth" (Genesis 1:1). In order for God to do that, He had to exist *before* the beginning.

- **God is eternal.** God is not defined or confined by time. He always was and He always will be (Psalm 90:2). God is also *infinite* in that He is above and beyond His finite creation.

- **God is holy.** God is perfect (the Bible term is *righteous*). In the negative context, He has no evil in Him; in the positive context, He is completely pure (Isaiah 6:3).

- **God is unchangeable.** Unlike the gods of other religions, God does not change. He is not capricious (that is, unpredictable). He is the same yesterday, today, and forever (Malachi 3:6).

- **God is just.** We don't have to worry that God won't be fair with everyone. God doesn't grade on the curve, and He doesn't play favorites (Revelation 15:3).

- **God is omnipotent.** God is all-powerful. No person, nation, or confederation—whether earthly or from the supernatural world—can conquer Him. God is able to do anything that is consistent with His nature (Revelation 19:6).

- **God is omniscient.** God knows everything about everything. There's nothing He doesn't know, including the details of your life, both good and bad (Proverbs 5:21).

- **God is omnipresent.** God is everywhere, but He is not in everything. God is not the universe; He exists apart from His creation. Yet there is never a time when He is not near to you (Psalm 139:7-12). This quality of God in which He is apart from and independent of anything or anyone else is called *transcendence*.

- *God is love.* God's holiness and His justice demand a penalty for imperfection, or sin. Yet God's love motivates Him to reach out to us even when we reject Him. The greatest demonstration of God's love was when He sent Jesus, His only Son, to earth to die for our sins (John 3:16).

- *God is personal.* God did not create the universe like a clock maker makes a clock. He didn't wind it up, only to let it wind down on its own. God is personally involved in His creation, holding it together with His power. And He is personally interested in your life. God knows you more intimately and more completely than you can imagine (Psalm 139:1-4).

God Has Spoken

The main reason we know that God is personal is that God has communicated personally with His creation. Although there is much about God that we cannot possibly understand, He has not hidden Himself from us. God has spoken—and by that we mean God has *revealed* Himself—to us in two distinct ways. Theologians refer to God's *general* and *special* revelation:

- *God's general revelation*—One of the most powerful and immediate ways God has spoken is through the universe itself. The intricate design and delicate balance of the universe is like a message from God that He exists and that He cares about us. The Bible says:

  From the time the world was created, people have seen the earth and sky and all that God made. They can clearly see his invisible qualities—his eternal power and divine nature. So they have no excuse whatsoever for not knowing God (Romans 1:20).

As amazingly wonderful as His creation is and as much as it points to God's existence, we need more information. What does God expect of us? How do we get to know this personal God on a personal basis?

Can You Prove God Exists?

Because God is a spirit Being who exists apart from His creation, it's impossible to scientifically prove that God exists. In other words, you won't find God by looking into the heavens with a telescope. Yet God has given us plenty of evidence for His existence so that no one could ever say, "No one ever told me about God."

- The universal idea about God points to His existence. Why would every single person who ever lived think about the same thing unless it was already there?

- The notion that there must be a first cause for all other causes (something that science is now acknowledging) points to God.

- The universe didn't happen by itself, including the complex and intricate design that makes the universe work in the first place. Many leading scientists have concluded that there must have been an "intelligent designer" at work.

- And where did the basic human sense of right and wrong in every culture come from? Only a holy God could have planted this "moral code" deep inside of every human being.

None of these arguments prove God's existence like you can prove the law of gravity, but the weight of evidence points to God.

- *God's special revelation*—God knew that His created beings were a curious bunch (after all, He made us that way), so He took another step beyond creation itself. God communicated to His created beings by giving them His Word. At first God spoke directly to people, and then He inspired 40 different writers over a period of 1600 years to record His personal message to humankind. Over time

How Do We Know
The Bible Is God's Word?

Of all the holy books ever written, the Bible is the only one that says it was written by God Himself. How do we know for sure that this is true? The answer has to do with *canonicity* and *transmission*. *Canonicity* was the process scholars and church leaders used to recognize which books of the Bible were inspired by God. *Canon* is the word that describes the 66 books that make up the Bible (the word *canon* comes from the word *reed,* which was used as a measuring stick in ancient times). In order for a particular book to measure up to the standards of God's Word, it had to speak with the authority of God, be written by a prophet of God, have the authentic stamp of God, impact people with the power of God, and be accepted by the people of God. Every book in the Bible passed this test and was recognized as being divinely inspired by God.

Transmission describes the way the original sacred writings were brought from the original writers to present-day readers using the most practical and reliable methods possible. An important measurement of accuracy and reliability is the number of copies of ancient manuscripts that exist. In the original Greek (the language of the New Testament), more than 5000 manuscript portions of the New Testament have been preserved. In addition, there are many other historical documents written at the same time as the New Testament that confirm the claims of Scripture. Not every person, date, or fact in the Bible has been verified by outside sources, but many have, and not one has been shown to be false.

Then there's the astounding record of Bible prophecies. The Bible contains around 2500 prophecies. Of those, approximately 2000 have already been fulfilled to the letter with no errors (the remaining 500 concern events that have not yet occurred). The only explanation for this 100 percent accuracy rate is that God Himself made the predictions and then fulfilled them. There is no other possibility.

these written records were collected into a single book, which came to be known as the Bible.

The Bible is often called the Word of God for a very simple reason: That's what it is. The Bible isn't just some words *about* God. The Bible represents the very words of God Himself (Hebrews 1:1). The process God used to write the Bible is referred to as *inspiration,* which literally means to "breathe in." God breathed His words into the human writers through the Holy Spirit (2 Peter 1:21). If God does not (and cannot) lie, and if God wrote the Bible through the divine inspiration of the Holy Spirit, then you can trust the Bible as being completely true (Psalm 33:4).

Because it was written by God and contains the message of God for all people for all time, the Bible is the ultimate spiritual authority for Christianity. But the Bible is not the ultimate way God communicated with people. God created people in His image so they could have a relationship with Him. But that relationship was broken when the human race rebelled against God (it's all written down in the first two chapters of Genesis). So what was God to do? How could the relationship between a holy God and sinful people be reestablished? God had to speak again in a more powerful and personal way.

Jesus: The Answer to Our Problem

After humankind rebelled against its Creator, God had a choice: He could either wipe out the human race, or He could offer to save it. The Bible says that God chose to save His rebellious creatures in a very specific way:

> *For God so loved the world that he gave his only Son, so that everyone who believes in him will not perish but have eternal life* (John 3:16).

We have already said that Christianity is a religion built around the Person and work of Jesus Christ. In reality, Christianity is more than a *religion* about Jesus. More accurately, it's about a *relationship* with Jesus, whom God sent to earth to save humanity from spiritual death. That is the heart and soul of Christianity. This is where Christianity stands apart from every other cult, religion, and spiritual belief in the world. A Christian is one who believes and accepts the claims of Jesus:

1. *Jesus claimed to be God in human form.* Jesus didn't say He was like a god. He said that He *was* God (John 10:30). The people around Jesus knew exactly what He meant. His enemies understood this claim, and they sought to kill Him for it (John 5:18). The followers of Jesus understood this claim as well, and they were willing to die for it. The apostle Paul wrote, "For in Christ the fullness of God lives in a human body" (Colossians 2:9). This "Jesus is God" premise is the foundation of Christianity.

2. *Jesus claimed to rise from the dead and claims to be alive today.* Anybody can claim to be God, and many people have. Some religions even propose that we can all become God. But where's the proof? A claim like that is ridiculous unless you can back it up. The same goes for Jesus. His claim to be God wouldn't have meant a thing unless He could prove it to the world, which is exactly what He did. While Jesus walked the earth, He offered several proofs for His divine nature: He performed incredible miracles that defied nature; He forgave sins, which only God can do; and He received the verbal endorsement from God the Father that Jesus was His Son (Matthew 3:16-17).

As important as these miraculous proofs were, they would have meant nothing if Jesus had not risen from the dead. The Bible says that Jesus died for our sins so that we could be made right with God (Romans 5:8-10). But without the resurrection, even the death of Jesus would have been pointless, and the faith of nearly two billion Christians living today wouldn't be worth a thing. The apostle Paul understood this when he wrote:

> *And if Christ has not been raised, then your faith is useless, and you are still under condemnation for your sins. In that case, all who have died believing in Christ have perished! And if we have hope in Christ only for this life, we are the most miserable people in the world* (1 Corinthians 15:17-19).

Jesus the Messiah

Throughout the Old Testament, God promised the Jews that He would send a king who would establish God's kingdom on earth. This "deliverer" was referred to as the Messiah. He would be God coming down to earth. There were nearly a hundred prophecies about this Messiah, and they were very specific. Jesus claimed to be the long-awaited Messiah. He fulfilled each prediction to the letter and lived His life to prove that He was, in fact, who He claimed to be. Unfortunately, the religious Jewish leaders failed to see that Jesus came to build a spiritual kingdom, not a political one. They failed to understand the words of their own prophets proclaiming that the Messiah would come to die for their sins (see Isaiah 53), rather than deliver them from political oppression. The religious leaders opposed Jesus because He pointed out their hypocritical religiosity. He said that a relationship with God was a matter of the inner heart, rather than outward performance.

The good news for Christians is that Jesus Christ did indeed rise from the dead. The resurrection is a fact expressed in the Bible (1 Corinthians 15:12), and it's a fact of history as well. Of all the great spiritual leaders and teachers who have ever lived, not one ever rose from the dead, and not one ever claimed that he would come back from the dead. Only Jesus made this claim and then made it happen. And since this is true, Jesus is alive today preparing a place in heaven for those who believe in Him (John 14:1-2). Not only that, but Jesus told His followers that He would be coming back to earth again someday to take all believers to heaven (John 14:3-4).

3. *Jesus invites His followers to enjoy a daily relationship with Him on earth.* In addition to offering an eternal relationship with

God in heaven, Jesus made it possible for His followers to enjoy a moment-by-moment personal relationship with Him on earth. No other religion proposes this sort of amazing familiarity with the founder. Everyone who accepts God's offer of salvation through Jesus can be in intimate contact with God. The Bible teaches that this personal, ongoing relationship with God is made possible by the Holy Spirit, the third Person in the Godhead. Jesus told His followers that when He left the earth, He would ask God to send the Holy Spirit, "who leads into all truth" (John 14:17). The Holy Spirit dwells in the life of all Christians, reminding them about Jesus and guiding them into the truth of God's Word.

The Mystery of the Three-in-One

Christianity is unique among all religions in its belief in the Trinity, which describes the three-in-one nature of God. The word *Trinity* doesn't appear in the Bible, but it is an important part of who God is and a foundational doctrine of Christianity. *Trinity* does not mean there are three gods who exist together to make up one God. There is only one God, but within that unity are three eternal and coequal Persons: God the Father, Jesus Christ the Son, and the Holy Spirit. All share the same essence and substance, but each has a distinct existence.

God Has Spoken—Humanity Must Respond

God has spoken to people through His creation, through His written Word, and through the living Word, Jesus Christ (John 1:1). There's nothing more that God needs to do to reconnect with His created beings. There is, however, something people must do in order to make the connection with God complete: They must respond. Unlike some other religions, Christianity does not teach that all people will eventually go to heaven. Nor does Christianity teach that they can earn their salvation through good works. Christianity is unique among world religions in its belief that salvation is God's gift to humanity, and people can accept it only by faith in Jesus Christ, the only way to God (Ephesians 2:8-9; Romans 10:9-10).

Dr. Hazen Adds...
A Confirming Miracle

The importance of the central miracle of Christianity, the physical resurrection of Jesus, simply cannot be minimized. It is nearly impossible to explain the rise and early success of the church without it. And the objective evidence is so strong in favor of this event that if we want to say it did not happen, we must first throw out everything we know about classical antiquity. This is because the evidence in favor of most other events of ancient history pales in comparison to the evidence for the life, death, and resurrection of Jesus of Nazareth. It is the objective evidence for this confirming miracle that sets Christianity apart from the other religions in a dramatic way. Christianity is truly testable.

Each person who accepts the gift of salvation through Jesus then becomes a member of the spiritual body of Christ (1 Corinthians 12:13), commonly known as the church.

Church: Why Bother?

In a book called *Church: Why Bother?* Phillip Yancey asks the question, "Why are there so many more professing Christians than churchgoing Christians?" He goes on to describe how difficult it is to sort out the church's human failings with the idealized concept of the church as the body of Christ. Many people share Yancey's struggle. They know church is important, but they don't like all of the disagreements and petty arguments that seem to divide one church from another. So they proudly call themselves Christians but stay away from church like the plague.

As we conclude this chapter, we will do our best to explain the purpose of the church and why it's important to Christianity. We also want to give you a quick overview of the history of the church—and Christianity—from the first century to today.

What Is the Church?

Before there was the Baptist Church, the Church of Christ, the Little Church in the Pines, or the Holy Spirit Catholic Church, there was simply the *church*. Actually, there is still just one church, even with all the various branches, denominations, and sects you see in every part of the world.

Wayne Grudem defines the church as "the community of all true believers for all time." Community is important to God. In effect, God exists in community through the Trinity, and God created us in His image to be in community first with Him and then with each other.

By Grudem's definition, the church has always been around. It did not originate with Jesus. What Jesus did was to establish a new community of believers made up of Jews descended from Abraham and the old covenant (the old agreement God had with His people, the Jews) and Gentiles (that is, non-Jews) who had one thing in common: belief in Jesus Christ as the basis of the new covenant (God's new agreement with all people).

The apostle Paul, whose dramatic conversion to Christianity turned him from the church's greatest enemy into the world's greatest missionary, described the church, otherwise known as the body of Christ, this way:

> *The human body has many parts, but the many parts make up only one body. So it is with the body of Christ. Some of us are Jews, some are Gentiles, some are slaves, and some are free. But we have all been baptized into Christ's body by one Spirit, and we have all received the same Spirit* (1 Corinthians 12:12-13).

Jesus Launches the Church

Paul and every other person who has ever committed his or her life to Jesus Christ by faith has been commissioned to be a missionary. Don't just think of a missionary as someone who wears a pith helmet and lives in a jungle somewhere. All Christians have a mission given by Jesus Himself moments before He ascended into heaven:

> *But when the Holy Spirit has come upon you, you will*
> *receive power and will tell people about me everywhere—*
> *in Jerusalem, throughout Judea, in Samaria, and to the ends*
> *of the earth* (Acts 1:8).

Within 50 days of this commission, the Holy Spirit came upon the believers in power, just as Jesus had predicted, and the church we know today was born. From that point on, the apostles and believers went out to bring the message of Christianity to people everywhere. Despite the intense persecution of the early Christians by the Roman government (or perhaps, *because* of the persecution), the church grew as the Good News (the gospel) reached the ends of the earth.

The Church Grows and Then Splits

As the church grew, various *heresies* (erroneous views) threatened to undermine the truth about Jesus as the only way to God. Thanks to the work of men like Justin Martyr and Irenaeus

Peter the Rock

The Gospel of Matthew records a conversation between Jesus and the apostle Peter that has become the basis for the church (see Matthew 16:17-19). Jesus asked His disciples, "Who do you say I am?" Peter answered, "You are the Messiah, the Son of the living God." Jesus then told Peter, "Now I say to you that you are Peter, and upon this rock I will build my church." One interpretation of this remarkable pronouncement is that Jesus made Peter the founder and first pope of the church. More likely, Jesus was declaring that Peter's pronouncement was to become the foundation upon which Christ would build His church. Indeed, Peter was the founder of the church in Jerusalem, where the Christian church began, but he never ruled the church with anything approaching papal authority.

(defenders of the faith known as *apologists*), the central truths of Christianity remained intact through the third century A.D. By the second century, the church founded by the apostles became the universal Catholic Church (headquartered in Rome), and in A.D. 312 the emperor Constantine, who converted to Christianity, put an end to all persecution of Christians.

Christianity became the dominant religion of the Roman Empire (that's what happens when the head guy converts), but eventually the church was divided into five regions: four in the East and Rome in the West. Because the Roman Church insisted on maintaining authority over Christians everywhere, a major split occurred in 1054 between the Roman Church and the four Eastern regions, creating the Roman Catholic Church in the West and the Orthodox Church in the East.

Dissension in the Ranks

While the Eastern Orthodox Church believed that the authority of the church needed to continue through "apostolic succession," the Roman Catholic Church built its authority on the *papacy*. The Roman Church believed that the apostle Peter was the first pope, followed by an unbroken succession of popes, each one acting as a "vicar" (or substitute) for Christ on earth. Catholics believed and continue to believe that the pope is infallible when he speaks *ex cathedra* (with authority).

The Roman Catholic Church grew to such prominence that it dominated both the cultural and political life of Western Europe. Great cathedrals and universities were built by the Church from the eleventh to the fourteenth centuries, but there was also great internal corruption and infighting.

By the fourteenth century, several prominent people were openly disagreeing with the Roman Church and calling for reform. John Wycliffe, an English reformer, boldly questioned papal authority, Church hierarchies, and other Catholic practices. He believed that the way to overcome what he perceived to be abusive authority was to make the Bible available to the people in their own language. Wycliffe was convinced that if people could read Scripture for themselves, they would understand how they could have a personal relationship with Jesus Christ without going through the Church. He was the first to translate the Latin Bible into English.

The Crusades

One of the most controversial periods in the history of the church started in 1095, when Western European Christians launched a series of wars—known as the *Crusades*—to recapture Jerusalem and the Holy Land, then controlled by the Muslims. The Crusades lasted well into the thirteenth century and were eventually expanded to include any military effort against non-Christians.

Martin Luther Nails It

Initially the reformers didn't want to separate from the Roman Catholic Church. They simply wanted to reform it from within, primarily by changing the Church's teaching on salvation. The Catholic Church believed that "you get to Christ through the Church." By contrast, the reformers believed that "you get to the Church through Christ."

The reformers' strongest statement came in 1517, when a German professor of theology by the name of Martin Luther published his 95 theses (tradition holds that he nailed them to the door of Castle Church in Wittenberg). Among other things, Luther protested the Catholic practice of indulgences, which were like favors or pardons for sin granted by the Church in exchange for payment or good works. Luther believed that pardon for sin came through faith alone *(sola fide)*. He also believed that the Bible alone *(sola scriptura)* is the source of final authority and truth.

Luther and his beliefs became the catalyst for the Reformation, which spread throughout Europe. Because the reformers were seen as protesting the teaching and practices of the Catholic Church, they eventually became known as Protestants. Over time *Protestantism* became a general term for a new set of traditions, which led to various churches—such as the Anglican Church in England, the Episcopal Church in America, and a host of Methodist, Baptist, Congregational, Presbyterian, Quaker, and Pentecostal churches and denominations.

What's That Again?

1. The one thing that sets Christianity apart from all the other cults, religions, and belief systems in the world is Jesus.

2. When comparing religions, it's important to start with Christianity because it's the only belief system that's testable.

3. Christianity is completely true in what it says about God and the supernatural world, and it's completely true to the way things are in the natural world.

4. The God of Christianity is a real spirit Being with personal characteristics.

5. The God of Christianity has spoken through His creation (general revelation) and His written Word (special revelation).

6. Christianity is all about a relationship with Jesus, who claimed and proved He was God in human form.

7. The church is defined as those who believe in God as revealed in the Scriptures and who unite to worship and serve Him.

8. Jesus commissioned the early believers to take the message of Christianity throughout the world.

9. The three main branches of Christianity are Eastern Orthodoxy, Roman Catholicism, and Protestantism.

Dig Deeper

Basic Christianity by John R.W. Stott is a classic book on just what the title implies. Dr. Stott has a way of explaining things clearly without watering them down.

On the other end of the understandability scale is Francis Schaeffer's *The God Who Is There*. You'll need your highlighter and thinking cap to plow through this great book, but it will be worth it.

Systematic Theology by Wayne Grudem devotes five chapters to the nature, purpose, power, and government of the church.

We found our own *Knowing God 101* to be very helpful in tracking the major beliefs about God, the Bible, Jesus, and all of the other major Christian doctrines.

■ ■ ■

Questions for Reflection and Discussion

1. Do you think it's a good idea to start this book with Christianity? What are the advantages? What are the disadvantages?

2. From your general knowledge of world religions (and without looking ahead in the book), give a true statement from each of these popular religions and cults: Islam, Mormonism, Jehovah's Witnesses, and Hinduism.

3. What does it mean when we say Christianity is *completely* true? Give two examples.

4. In what ways has God communicated with His creation? What's the difference between general and special revelation? Can someone be saved by general revelation? Why or why not?

5. In what ways is the Bible unique among the holy books of the other world religions and cults? Why can you trust the Bible to be reliable?

6. Explain why the resurrection of Jesus Christ is the most important event of Christianity. How does this event separate Christianity from other religions and cults?

7. How has the church been able to survive from the first century to today?

■ ■ ■

Moving On . . .

Just as you can't define Christianity without Jesus Christ, you can't fully appreciate it without Judaism, the religion of God's chosen people, the Jews. Why? Because Jesus was a Jew, descended from the royal Jewish line of David, and because Jesus came to earth first as the Messiah to the Jews.

God hasn't forgotten His people, and neither should you. In the next chapter we'll explore Judaism, the world's first and oldest monotheistic religion.

*C*hapter 2

Jews are like everybody else,
only more so.

Howland Spencer

Christianity and Judaism share the same origins, so we thought we already knew a lot about Judaism. But that was before we did our research for this chapter. While we are a little embarrassed to admit it, our prior impressions and understandings of Judaism were based mainly on its customs and practices of 3000 years ago, like animal sacrifices and pilgrimages in the desert. As far as contemporary Judaism is concerned, about all we knew were the names of Jews who had attained celebrity status, whether in science (Albert Einstein), diplomacy (Henry Kissinger), or entertainment (Steven Spielberg).

Maybe it will come as no surprise to you that Judaism is much more than ancient rituals or famous personalities. It has both, and each gives a clue to this faith that is steeped in historical and cultural heritage. But the legacy of Judaism often results in social and political controversies that are not associated with other religions. As we learned, Judaism has always been at the center of geopolitical disputes, whether the Jews wanted them or not. When a faith always seems to be the center of controversy, it merits investigation.

Judaism:
A Chosen People, Place, and Purpose

hat's *A*head

- [ ] The Genesis of Judaism
- [ ] It's All About the Rules, but It's Not About the Rules
- [ ] Everything You Need to Know About Sects
- [ ] A Religion, a Race, or Something Else?
- [ ] Persecution Plus

*W*hat are your thoughts of Judaism? Are they based on your role as villager #3 in your high school production of *Fiddler on the Roof?* Or maybe you have been moved by the tragedy and horror of the Holocaust by watching *Schindler's List*. Maybe you are a bit envious that the traditional gift-giving celebration of Hanukkah extends over seven days, as opposed to your single-day event of Christmas. If your impressions of Judaism are based on such isolated notions, you need to wipe your mental slate clean and start over. The essence of this religion involves devotion and destiny that impacts daily life.

The Genesis of Judaism

Judaism is the religion of the Jews. It was the first great faith to believe in one God. The ancestry of the religion begins with Abraham, whose story is recorded in the book of Genesis. The story of Abraham is all about a promise (called a covenant). God's promise to Abraham involved...

- *A people*—God told Abraham that he would be the father of a great nation.

  Look up into the heavens and count the stars if you can. Your descendants will be like that—too many to count! (Genesis 15:5).

  This promise really becomes amazing when you realize that God said it to Abraham while he and his wife were childless and about 70 years old!

- *A place*—God promised Abraham and his descendants a homeland.

  Yes, I will give all this land of Canaan to you and to your offspring forever (Genesis 17:8).

  The land of Canaan is the region now known as Israel and Palestine.

- *A purpose*—There was a reason behind God's promise. It included the purpose of using Abraham and his descendants to teach all the people of the world about the one true God.

  All the families of the earth will be blessed through you (Genesis 12:3).

As a result of this covenant with the descendants of Abraham, the Jews (referred to originally as Hebrews or Israelites) have been called "God's chosen people."

This isn't some accolade that they slapped on themselves undeservedly. It dates back to Moses, who gave a speech to the Hebrew people that included this famous line:

For you are a holy people, who belong to the Lord your God. Of all the people on earth, the Lord your God has chosen you to be his own special treasure. The Lord did not choose you and lavish his love on you because you were larger or greater than other nations, for you were the smallest of all nations! It was simply because the LORD *loves you, and because he was keeping the oath he had sworn to your ancestors* (Deuteronomy 7:6-8).

A Quick Look at Judaism

- There are about 18 million Jews throughout the world. (Precise statistics are difficult to obtain because many nations don't keep track of such things, and not every Jew chooses to admit such things, particularly in countries where Jews are persecuted.)

- The population of Jews increased in the last two centuries. At the time of the Revolutionary War, the Jewish population in America was about 2000. By the time of the Civil War, there were about 300,000 Jews living in America. The current Jewish population in America is about seven million.

- After the United States, the next largest concentration of Jews is found in Israel (about five million).

- A Gallup poll reported that Jews are less religious than other Americans. While 69 percent of the general American population claimed membership in a church, only 44 percent of American Jews reported belonging to a synagogue. In the week of the survey, 40 percent of the general population attended a religious service, but only 21 percent of the Jews reported attending their synagogue.

- Prior to 1965, only 11 percent of American Jews had married a non-Jew. Since 1985, the percentage has increased to over 50 percent.

The Messiah Mystery

There is a messianic aspect to Judaism. For centuries Jews have been awaiting the arrival of the Messiah—the promised "greater prophet"—who would bring about the blessings on Abraham's people according to God's original covenant. Part of the "chosen" aspect of the Jews is the fact that God will bring a Messiah to the earth through Abraham's bloodline. This Messiah will not only be a Savior for the Jews, but he will also be a blessing to all humanity, according to God's promise to Abraham.

The exact identity of the Messiah was never given, but all throughout the Tenakh (the Old Testament) there are promises of a coming king who will establish God's kingdom on earth. Scholars have found more than 40 clues in the sacred writings that give specific information about the Messiah, including where He would be born, His family lineage, events of His life, and the circumstances of His death.

Over the past 4000 years since the time of Abraham, there have been many times when the Jews suffered from political persecution and eagerly desired the arrival of the Messiah, who would bring about a military revolt and victory. This was certainly the situation during the time of Jesus Christ, when the Jews suffered under the oppression of the Roman Empire. But Jesus didn't fit the prototype that the Jews were expecting. Some accepted Him as the Messiah based on prophecies that the Messiah would be a "suffering servant" and on the understanding that the new "kingdom" was spiritual instead of political. The Jewish officials at the time, however, ruled that Jesus was a Messiah impostor, and a decree was issued that there was to be no teaching about Jesus.

The Christian church was initially comprised of Jews who believed that Jesus was the Messiah. In the beginning, some Jesus-believing Jews even questioned whether a non-Jew could be a Christian. This very significant dispute impacted the development of Judaism, which then emphasized that Jesus was not the Messiah. There was a strong anti-Jesus sentiment born in Judaism that has resulted in discrimination and persecution of the Jews (as we'll discuss later in this chapter).

It has been 2000 years since the time of Jesus, and Judaism continues to await the Messiah. Over time, some Jews (in the Reform branch) have come to view the Messiah as a period of peace and prosperity rather than as an actual person.

The Ten Commandments . . . and a Lot More

God wanted to show the people of the world how to live according to His principles. It was His plan to use the Jews to demonstrate those principles. To start things off, God gave Moses the Ten Commandments. These rules form the basis for the covenant between God and the Jewish people, but they also constitute basic principles for how all of humanity should relate to God and each other. These commandments, also called the Decalogue (*Devarim* in Hebrew) can be summarized as follows:

1. You shall have no other gods to rival Me.

2. You shall not make yourself a carved image.

3. You shall not misuse the name of the Lord your God.

4. Remember the Sabbath day and keep it holy.

5. Honor your father and your mother.

6. You shall not kill.

7. You shall not commit adultery.

8. You shall not steal.

9. You shall not give false evidence against your neighbor.

10. You shall not covet.

But these are not all of the rules prescribed for a Jew's lifestyle. There are more—lots more. In fact, there are 613 *mitzvot* (commandments) in the sacred writings of Judaism. Some are affirmative commandments (things to do), some are negative ones (things not to do), and some can't be followed because they pertain to the Temple procedures (and the Temple doesn't currently exist).

Torah, Torah, Torah

The word *Torah* can mean different things in different contexts. Its most limited usage refers to the five books written by Moses: Genesis, Exodus, Leviticus, Numbers, and Deuteronomy. In a more general sense, *Torah* means the entire Jewish Bible (specifically referred to as the Tanakh, or Written Torah). In its broadest sense, _Torah_ refers to the entirety of Jewish law and teachings.

There are two primary sources for rules governing the worship and lifestyle of Judaism:

- **_The Written Torah_.** These are the 39 books that are known to Jews as the Tanakh and known to Christians as the Old Testament. (For Jews, there is no New Testament.) The books are compiled in a different order in the Tanakh than in the Old Testament. The first five books are "the Law" (the five books of Moses); the other 34 books are categorized as "the Prophets" and "the Writings."

- **_The Oral Torah_.** Orthodox Jews believe that God explained the meaning and interpretation of the written Torah to Moses. Moses, in turn, passed these teachings on to other people. These instructions were passed in oral form down through the generations until they were transcribed in about A.D. 200 in a book known as the _Mishnah_. Additional commentaries, called the _Gemara_, were written over the next several centuries to amplify and expand the Mishnah. The Mishnah and the Gemara are together known as the _Talmud_. The Talmud covers almost every aspect of life that you could encounter, including issues dealing with marriage, finances, business, agriculture, worship, lawsuits, and morality.

It's All About the Rules, but It's Not About the Rules

With the 613 commandments in the Written Torah and the comprehensive instructions in the Talmud, you might think that Judaism is rigid and confining. Yes, there are rules governing every aspect of life (including what to eat, what to wear, how to act, what to say, and who to marry), but Judaism is more about _relationships_ than it is about _rules_. Those relationships include...

- the connection between God and humanity

- God's specific and special affiliation with the Jews

- the sense of ownership that the Jews have for their promised homeland

- the special bond between Jews

- interpersonal relationships among all people

Instead of viewing their religion as a long list of do's and don'ts, Jews consider the principles given by God and those instituted by the rabbis as long-standing customs that enhance these relationships.

The attitude of Jews toward their laws and customs is better understood by examining the word *halakhah*. This word is often translated to mean "Jewish law." But the literal meaning of the word is "the path that one walks." The root words for *halakhah* mean "to go, to walk, or to travel."

Traditional Judaism is not merely legalistic. It is not a religion that is so full of rules and rituals that it lacks emotion or spirituality. Instead, the halakhah is intended to increase the spirituality in a person's life. As one Jewish commentator has said, halakhah "turns the most trivial, mundane acts, such as eating and getting dressed, into acts of religious significance."

There is not universal agreement within Judaism regarding how strictly these rules must be followed. Some Jews believe that the principles are absolute and unchanging laws from God. Others say that the laws from God can change and evolve over time according to the interpretation of the rabbis. Still other Jews consider the principles to be guidelines that can be followed or ignored as a person chooses. Nonetheless, the prevailing opinion recognizes that the observance of the halakhah increases a sense of spirituality and the influence of religion on one's life. Living life according to these principles and customs will continually remind you of your faith and connect you in a more meaningful way with God.

Everything You Need to Know About Sects

Judaism isn't big on dogma. For the Jews, their belief system is loose enough to let each person formulate his or her own doctrine. For them, actions are more important than a formulaic statement of faith. That's why there is a Jewish expression that says, "Ask three rabbis, and you'll get five different opinions."

If there is one overriding doctrinal truth of Judaism, it takes the form of the *Shema,* which faithful Jews are supposed to recite twice daily: "Hear, O Israel: The Lord is our God, the Lord is one."

The closest thing to a widely accepted explanation of the tenets of Judaism is found in the 13 principles written by the Jewish rabbi and scholar Moses Maimonides (A.D. 1135–1204). These are what he considered to be the basics of the Jewish faith:

1. God exists and is the sole Creator.

2. There is only one, unique God.

3. God has no bodily form or shape.

4. God is eternal.

5. We should pray to God and to Him only.

6. The words of the prophets are true.

7. The prophecies of Moses are true, and he is the greatest of the prophets.

8. The Written Torah (the five books of the Tanakh) and the Oral Torah (the teachings of the Talmud) are true.

9. The Torah is not subject to change, and there will never be another Torah from God.

10. God knows the thoughts and deeds of every person.

11. God will reward those who are good and will punish those who are wicked.

12. The Messiah will come.

13. The dead will be resurrected.

Contrary to many religions (and certainly the other two monotheistic religions, Christianity and Islam), Judaism isn't fixed on certain cosmological or metaphysical beliefs. While this religion doesn't ignore the nature of God, humanity, the universe, and the afterlife, there is no official position on these subjects (except perhaps as enumerated by Maimonides, and Jews can even waffle on those concepts).

The Big Three

Judaism is more concerned about a person's actions than a person's beliefs. The freedom allowed for personal opinion in the abstract issues of their theology and the importance placed on personal behavior is reflected in the three major sects (divisions or movements) within Judaism.

All Jews are not alike. They are categorized by the way they respond to the halakhah's ordinances for personal action and behavior:

- *The Orthodox Jew.* This is the oldest and most conservative branch of Judaism. They consider themselves to be "Torah-true." An orthodox Jew strictly adheres to the original form of Judaism, with all of its customs and practices. Every word of the sacred texts is considered to be divinely inspired and mandatory.

- *The Reform Jew.* This is the liberal and more permissive side of Judaism, followed by many North American Jews. The movement began in the 1790s in Germany. A Reform Jew (not reform*ed* Jew) follows the ethical laws of Judaism, but the other traditional customs (affecting such things as diet and apparel) are ignored. Worship is conducted in a temple instead of a synagogue. English can be used instead of Hebrew, and musical instruments are permitted. There is no gender segregation in worship, and there can be female rabbis in Reform congregations. Instructions from God are considered progressive and can be influenced by history and cultural changes.

- *The Conservative Jew.* Don't let the name fool you. It is not the most conservative branch of Judaism. It is sort of a compromise between the strict adherence of the Orthodox position and the permissive stance of the Reform view. It retains much of the traditions while making accommodations for contemporary lifestyles. Some of the dietary restrictions are followed, but not all of them. Worship is partly in Hebrew, partly in English.

Several Smaller Movements

Although the Orthodox, Reform, and Conservative movements are the largest forms of Judaism, there are several smaller groups:

- *Hasidic Judaism* began in the eighteenth century in Poland in response to the unemotional Judaism that existed at that time in Eastern Europe. The Hasidic ("pious") movement emphasizes joy and emotion in Judaism as opposed to book learning and intellectualism. Hasidic influence waned during the nineteenth century, but some groups still remain.

- *Humanistic Judaism* represents those Jews who espouse no formal religion. Many are atheists or agnostics. They take a moralistic approach to the ethical questions of life. They are Jews by culture and heritage, but they don't participate in any religious aspects of life.

- *Reconstructionism* is a radical group that began in 1934 with Mordecai Kaplan, who was excommunicated by the Union of Orthodox Rabbis. This movement views Judaism as a civilization instead of a religious community. Kaplan said that Jews are not God's chosen people (which explains why he is viewed with disfavor by traditional Jews).

- *Zionism* is a movement which seeks to colonize Jews in the land of Israel. It began in response to oppression of the Jews and a fear of loss of identity. Israel became an official nation in 1948, and citizenship was offered to any Jew in the world.

A Religion, a Race, or Something Else?

Judaism is the only major religion that was instituted within and for a specific bloodline (Abraham and his descendants). This peculiarity has led to some interesting apparent anomalies:

- Although Judaism is a religion, a Jew can be an atheist who believes there is no God.

- Although there is an official and common ancestry in Judaism, you might be considered an anti-Semite (being anti-Jewish) if you refer to the Jews as a separate race.

- A person who is outside the ancestry of Abraham (a "Gentile") can still be considered a Jew.

If you are asking how there can be such contradictions, we'll be glad to give you the answers. (Actually, we are giving you the answers whether you are asking or not.)

Can a Jew Be a Christian?

There are some Jews who believe that Jesus is the promised Messiah. They identify with the beliefs of Christianity, but they are culturally and ethnically Jews. Instead of being called Christians, they might prefer the designation of *Messianic Jew* or *Hebrew Christian*. (Others consider *Messianic Jew* to be confusing since traditional Judaism includes a messianic expectation.)

Within traditional Judaism, a Jew who accepts Jesus as the Messiah (i.e., becomes a Christian) is no longer considered a Jew. Christianity and Judaism are considered to be mutually exclusive. The Israeli Supreme Court has ruled that Jews who believe in Jesus as the Messiah are not "Jews" under the law, which grants citizenship to all Jews.

Most Jews who believe that Jesus is the Messiah do not want to renounce their Jewish heritage. They consider themselves to be *completed* or *fulfilled* Jews because their Messiah has already come.

Judaism Is a Religion . . . but Not Only That

There definitely is a religion of Judaism. Yes, there is a lot of latitude for individual beliefs, but Judaism is an official, organized religion. You can look it up in the religious encyclopedias. It is taught as a major world religion in the universities around the world. It has a history and sacred writings. Its synagogues and temples exist in almost every country.

But it is not just a religion. There are many Jews who have no belief in God. (Some data exist to indicate that more than half of the Jews living in Israel today consider themselves humanistic or secular Jews who have no belief in God or in any religious aspect of Judaism.) Many Jews may participate in cultural customs and rituals, but they do so out of a sense of heritage rather than from any spiritual motivation. These nonreligious individuals are still considered Jews (even by most traditional and orthodox movements). A Jew isn't excluded from Judaism simply because he or she has no spiritual faith. Therefore, Judaism must be more than a religion.

The Jews Are a Race . . . but Not Really

Following the civil rights movement of the 1960s, the U.S. Supreme Court issued a decision declaring that Jews are a "race" for purposes of certain antidiscrimination laws. For most people, this decision was not controversial. Just as most people at that time referred to African-Americans as a "race," Jews were considered a race. What other group of people could trace their ancestry back 4000 years to a single individual? Moreover, almost since its inception, Judaism had required that Jews marry only another Jew. For the most part, this rule was followed, and the bloodline remained distinct.

Somewhat surprisingly, many Jews objected to being categorized as a separate race by the Supreme Court. Many Jews living at that time could still remember the claims made a few decades earlier in Nazi Germany that the Jews were an inferior race. But beyond this visceral reaction, there was also a scientific objection to the categorization of the Jews as a race. Race is determined by genetic distinctions and shared ancestry. It is a matter of the imprint of a person's DNA.

There is no DNA requirement to become a Jew. Yes, there is a shared ancestry among many Jews, but Judaism is not genetically exclusive. Any person from any ethnic origin or nationality or ancestry can become a Jew by conversion. Take comedian Adam Sandler, now-deceased entertainer Sammy Davis, Jr., and news reporter Connie Chung. This group represents three Jews, yet there are three separate races represented in the group as well.

There is even more cultural and ethnic diversity among Jews than most people realize. Take, for example, Yiddish idioms (such as *chutzpah,* meaning "shameless audacity," or *nebbish,* which can be loosely translated as "nerdish"). These terms are well-known to *Ashkenazic* Jews (those with cultural roots from Eastern Europe, as are most American Jews). But such terminology may be unknown in the Jewish communities in Africa. Similarly, foods that you might automatically associate as being Jewish (such as lox and bagels) will be totally foreign to *Sephardic* Jews in Portugal. Judaism transcends any single culture or ethnic group.

The Jews Are a Nation, but Not the Kind You Think

The Torah gives the best categorization of the Jews. It refers to them as a nation. The Hebrew word used in the Torah is *goy*. Although *goy* is literally translated as our English word *nation*, the exact meaning has nothing to do with a geographical boundary line or the country of Israel on the eastern edge of the Mediterranean Sea. *Goy* refers to a group of people with a shared sense of common history, destiny, and purpose. *Goy* conveys the sense of universal connectedness that is enjoyed by Jews.

Jews may be reluctant to describe their commonality by the word *nation.* They don't want to be viewed as disloyal to the country of their residence or citizenship. So they might describe themselves as "the Jewish people" or the "children of Israel" (which is a reference to Abraham's grandson, Jacob, who was also known as Israel). However it is described, Jews throughout history and around the world have acknowledged a common sense of identity with each other, whether they are Jews by ancestral descent or by conversion.

Persecution Plus

Oppression and persecution of the Jews didn't start and end with the Nazi concentration camps and death chambers during World War II. The Jews have suffered hatred, harassment, and cruelty throughout their history. Much of the time they did nothing to merit such treatment except hold true to their faith.

- The Tanakh includes historical accounts of the invasions by the Assyrians and the Babylonians when Jews were

taken captive from the Promised Land and enslaved in
other parts of the world about 2500 years ago.

- About 1000 years ago during the Crusades, Christians in
  Europe sought to liberate the Holy Land from Muslim dom-
  ination. The religious fervor extended to Jews. The Cru-
  saders reasoned that it was ridiculous to go to a distant
  land and kill Muslims without also killing the Jews who
  were also God's enemy because they opposed Christianity.
  In central Europe more than 10,000 Jews were killed, and
  more were murdered within the Holy Land.

- About 500 years ago, anti-Semitism arose during the
  Spanish Inquisition. King Ferdinand and Queen Isabella
  signed an expulsion edict that gave Jews four months to
  convert to Christianity or leave the country.

- Even Martin Luther, the great Christian reformer, outlined
  a plan in 1543 for dealing with the Jews for their blasphemy against Christ. His plans included burning their
  synagogues, destroying their homes, and confiscating their
  wealth.

Things aren't much different today. Some people who claim
to be Christians are opposed to the Jews because they fail to recognize Jesus as the Messiah. In the Arab world, the Jews are despised
because they claim rights to what they consider to be the Promised
Land that was given by God to their ancestor Abraham.

The Beliefs of Judaism

What About...	According to Judaism...
God	He is the powerful Ruler of the universe. He is loving and just. There is a tension between the nearness and the farness of God, but humanity can communicate with Him.
Humanity	People are basically good because they were created in the image of God. They have the ability to make ethical choices. They are responsible for their actions.
Sin	Although people have a good nature, they have an evil inclination that may lead them astray.
Salvation and the Afterlife	The concept of an afterlife is not well-developed. Your eternal existence is determined by your moral behavior and attitudes. God offers forgiveness to those who repent and atone for their sins through positive action. You are responsible for leading a moral life while here on earth; any judgment in the afterlife is best left to God.
Morals	The desired patterns for behavior are addressed in the literature of Judaism. Morality is based upon the good of the community and social justice. Marriage and children are valued.
Worship	This is a major part of life. Rituals and ceremony play an important role. Jewish worship is prayer-centered.
Jesus	Some recognize that He was a great teacher of morality. Most consider Him to be an impostor Messiah.

What's That Again?

1. Judaism is a monotheistic religion, believing in one all-powerful God who created the universe and everything in it.

2. God chose Abraham and his descendants as a "chosen people" to reveal God's principles for living to the rest of the world. God gave to the Jews the Promised Land and promised a Messiah who would bring peace and prosperity to the Jews.

3. The sacred writings of Judaism set forth rules for conduct and personal behavior in all areas of life.

4. Actions are more important than beliefs.

5. The traditional view holds that Jesus was not the promised Messiah. While many Jews still await the Messiah's arrival, others don't expect a personal Messiah but are expecting peacefulness in a messianic age.

6. Although there is strong ancestral heritage among Jews, a non-Jew can convert to the religion of Judaism.

Dig Deeper

Look for the *Reader's Digest* publication entitled *The World's Religions: Understanding the Living Faiths*. It gives an excellent overview of ten major world religions, including Judaism.

Several doctrinal points of Judaism are compared with other religions at www.leaderu.com. Go to the world religions index.

You can find a list of the 613 mitzvot (commandments) from the Torah at www.jewfaq.com. This website, known as Judaism 101, is an excellent online encyclopedia of Judaism.

In his book *How to Respond to Judaism*, Erwin J. Kolb explains doctrinal and cultural issues that may be important to consider if you are in a religious discussion with someone of the Jewish faith.

■ ▓ ▓

*Q*uestions for *R*eflection and *D*iscussion

1. When you compare Judaism with Christianity, do you think the beliefs they share in common are greater or less than their differences?

2. Do you agree that people are basically good because they were created in God's image? Defend your answer.

3. From the people you know of the Jewish faith, do you have a sense that they are still awaiting the arrival of the Messiah, or does that seem unimportant to them?

4. Why might the term "Jews for Jesus" or "Christian Jew" be offensive to a person who adheres to a more traditional form of Judaism?

5. In what ways is Judaism like a religion, and in what ways is it not?

6. Why do you suppose that the Jews have been such a target for persecution?

7. As far as individual personal faith is concerned, which is more important: beliefs or conduct?

◼ ◻ ◻

Moving On . . .

You don't have to be a winner on *Jeopardy* or a reporter for CNN to know that there is constant military conflict in the Middle East. Much of the tension arises from the hatred between Muslims and Jews. It isn't all about politics. Much of it has to do with opposing religious perspectives. You have just finished an overview of Judaism. Now it is time to gain some insights into the Islamic point of view.

Chapter 3

O God! Whatever share of this world you have allotted to me, bestow it on your enemies; and whatever share of the next world you have allotted to me, bestow it on your friends. You are enough for me.

Rabi'a al-Adawiyya

We don't know about you (obviously), but the continuing military tension and conflict in the Middle East never weighed heavily on us. It was halfway around the world, and we were not directly—or even remotely—involved. We knew that part of the problem involved land disputes, but the differences between the Jews and the Muslims appeared to be at the heart of it. We knew a little bit about Judaism, but far less about the Islamic faith. Our lack of knowledge didn't bother us because we weren't even curious about Islam.

But then the events of September 11, 2001, got our attention. Along with most other Americans, we suddenly had an urgent desire to find out as much as we could about Muslims. We heard reports out of Afghanistan that Americans were the targets of a holy war. Militant Muslims referred to us (Americans—not Bruce and Stan) as infidels who must be wiped off the face of the earth in accordance with the teachings of Muhammad. Other Muslims, however, proclaimed that Islam was a religion of peace and that terrorist attacks were the work of Islamic fundamentalists who were perverting the true teachings of the Muslim faith.

We think you'll be surprised to find out what Islam is all about. We were.

Islam:
It's All About Allah

Difference between Jesus & Allah is Love

*W*hat's *A*head

- ☐ Mystical Meditations in Mecca
- ☐ Standing on the Five Doctrines
- ☐ Leaning on the Five Pillars
- ☐ The Sunni–Shi'ite Split

*I*f we were designing and starting a religion, we would probably include a lot of hoopla and fanfare for publicity purposes. Hey, with all of the different religions competing for your devotion, we would have to draw a little attention to our new one. We might try holding a press conference with fireworks. We could kick things off by distributing free religious T-shirts to the first one million adherents. We would try anything flashy to get people to notice the new religion we were promoting.

So we find it interesting that the three monotheistic religions all involved humble beginnings. (Maybe that happens when a religion begins a few thousand years ago in the desert of the Middle East. There wasn't much to work with at that time, except sand.)

- With Judaism, Abraham was fairly wealthy, but God treated him like a nomadic Bedouin by moving him around in search of the Promised Land.

- The central figure of Christianity, Jesus, was born in a stable with the scent of sheep manure and shepherd sweat in the air.

- And it wasn't much better at the start of Islam...

Mystical Meditations in Mecca

The year was A.D. 570 when Muhammad ibn Abdallah was born into an aristocratic family in Mecca (in what is now Saudi Arabia). But the circumstances for little Muhammad began bleakly and soon got worse. His father died before he was born, and that caused the family business to crumble. Then his mother died when he was six years old. Muhammad was shuffled off to live with his grandfather, but Grandpa died shortly thereafter. So young Muhammad moved in with his uncle, who was the head of the Quraish clan.

A Quick Look at Islam

- Islam is the second largest of the world's religions.

- There are more than one billion Muslims in the world.

- Being only 1400 years old (having started in the seventh century), Islam is the youngest of the major world religions.

- A growing Islamic presence in the United States did not begin until about the mid- to late-1800s. It is believed that the first mosque in the United States was constructed in 1934 in Cedar Rapids, Iowa.

- In compliance with their religious requirement to make a pilgrimage to Mecca at least once in a lifetime, more than two million Muslims annually visit Mecca in the twelfth month of the Muslim year.

Perhaps living with his uncle gave Muhammad some spiritual sensitivity (or maybe that came from the fact that people around him kept dying). The Quraish clan had the responsibility for the Ka'aba, a Meccan shrine and place of pilgrimage in Arabia. While there were Jews and Christians in the area (which exposed Muhammad to these religions), most of the residents of Mecca worshiped numerous gods and natural phenomena, such as trees and rocks. Going on pilgrimages and offering sacrifices were two of the main religious practices in the polytheistic culture around him.

Tradition says that Muhammad could neither read nor write. But he had a knack for commerce. At age 25, he married a 40-year-old woman who owned the caravan business that he was managing. The newlyweds made Mecca their home, and Muhammad was set to begin a successful business career. But as it turned out, Muhammad was more a thinker than a trader. He was disillusioned by the polytheistic and idolatrous practices around him. He often sought solitude in a cave outside Mecca.

In 610, when Muhammad was 40 years old, he was sitting in his cave when he received the first of a series of mystical visions that changed his life (and the world). Initially, Muhammad was unsure whether his visions were divine, but his wife was convinced that they were from God. Muhammad eventually believed that the archangel Gabriel delivered God's message to him—that there was only one true God and that idolatry was an abomination.

Who Was Muhammad's God?

Muhammad's God was known as "Al-Lah" (now more commonly *Allah*), a name that means "the God."

The Prophet Preaches and Dictates

For two years after Muhammad received his first visions, he kept quiet. Then in A.D. 612, he began to preach and started to get converts. He continued to receive revelations. Since he couldn't read or write, Muhammad recited these revelations to his disciples, who wrote them down.

Eventually these transcribed recitations were collected into a book called the Qur'an (which means "the reciting" or "the reading").

The Qur'an (sometimes spelled *Koran*) contains 114 chapters, referred to as *surahs*. The Qur'an is approximately four-fifths the length of the New Testament.

Although he was gaining a considerable following to his message of Allah, most of the people in Mecca were hostile to Muhammad's teachings. (This is another common trait shared by the monotheistic religions. Idolatrous and immoral people take offense at the teachings of a holy and moral God.) As Muhammad proclaimed his message that Allah opposed the arrogance and materialism of the people in Mecca, he started to make enemies. In 622, Muhammad and his small band of followers were forced to flee north to the city now known as Medina ("the city of the prophet").

The Prophet Battles and Conquers

Muhammad organized a small army to establish peace among the various fighting tribal groups in Medina. Through combat and diplomacy, he achieved stability in the region. He built a mosque and formed a government that set rules for the people in all areas of life: religious, economic, political, and social. Meanwhile, back in his hometown, the Meccans organized an army to destroy Muhammad and his followers. Major battles ensued over a six-year period, but in A.D. 630, Muhammad and his forces conquered the city of Mecca and destroyed every idol and shrine except the Kaaba (which became the most sacred place on earth to Muslims).

After the conquest of Mecca, Muhammad was able to extend his control over most of Arabia by treaty or by force. He was a

Mark Your Calendar

Muhammad's migration to Medina is referred to as the Hegira. Muslims hold the Hegira in such high regard that the year A.D. 622 marks the beginning of the Islamic calendar. The years since then are counted from "A.H.," meaning "the year of the Hegira."

combined religious leader and governmental ruler, enforcing the worship of Allah. Muhammad continued to reside in Medina, and he made his last pilgrimage to the Kaaba in March 632. He died three months later. After his death, his followers zealously carried their new faith across Asia, Africa, and into Europe.

An Abridged Islamic Lexicon

Muhammad founded the religion of Islam. *Islam* is an Arabic term meaning "submission" to the will of one God, Allah. The Arabic root word (much like the Hebrew root word for *shalom*) means "peace"—the peace and social accord that come from submitting to the will of God.

Those who submit to the will of Allah are referred to as *Muslims*. A *mumin* is one who just intellectually accepts the Islamic faith, but a *Muslim* is one who not only believes in the faith but also submits to the will of Allah by the practice of Islam in daily life (see the discussion of the Five Pillars on pages 73-74).

Muslims reject the term *Muhammadanism* because their faith is in Allah. Although Muhammad was the greatest prophet of Allah, Muhammad is not to be worshiped.

Standing on the Five Doctrines

There is always a risk of oversimplification in trying to summarize the beliefs of a religion. With most religions, it is difficult to reduce the major points of doctrine into, say, five simple categories. The task is easier with Islam, however, because it has five fundamental doctrines. Don't just scan the title to each category and think that you automatically know the doctrine. Although there are similar doctrinal categories in Judaism and Christianity, the specifics of the Islamic doctrine might be different than you would expect.

Doctrine #1: God

Muslims believe in the existence and preeminence of God. There is only one God, and his name happens to be Allah.

With the utterance of *Allah akbar* in their daily prayers, Muslims acknowledge that "God is greater than everything." They know him to be all-seeing, all-hearing, all-knowing, and all-powerful. The powers they attribute to Allah are the same as those famous "omni" attributes of the God of Judaism and Christianity:

- omniscience: all-knowing
- omnipotence: all-powerful
- omnipresence: everywhere at the same time

Any similarity with the views of Judaism and Christianity on the subject of God comes to a screeching halt at this point, however. The closer you examine the nature of Allah, the less he looks like the God of the Jews and the Christians.

- ### *What's Love Got to Do with It?*

  Muslims have "99 beautiful names" for Allah (which they memorize), and each one describes one of Allah's characteristics. Many non-Muslims believe that "love" is not one of Allah's 99 names, but the Qur'an does describe Allah as loving in at least two places. However, this is not a defining characteristic. Allah's character is defined in the Qur'an more in terms of judgment than grace, and more in terms of power than mercy.

  When it comes to love, the overarching message of the Qur'an is that Allah's love is conditioned on the response of those who love him by doing good (meaning that they do good deeds and adhere to the required daily practices of the Five Pillars as discussed below). It seems that Allah does not love the person whose bad deeds outweigh the good things he or she has done.

  The attribute of love is a huge difference between Allah and the God of Judaism and Christianity. That's why it is incorrect to believe that Allah and God are the same deity but are simply known by two different names, depending upon whether you are sitting in a mosque or a church. But this isn't like calling a couch by alternative names such as divan, sofa, davenport, or loveseat. Allah of the Qur'an only loves those he deems to be good; the God of the Bible loves all of humanity, none of whom are basically good.

If anyone ever questions whether there is a difference between Allah and God, tell them love is the answer.

• *Getting to Know You*

Both Allah and God are described as being transcendent (meaning that they are above and beyond us in other dimensions of time and space). This characteristic fits with the Muslim concept that Allah is unknowable and incomprehensible.

> ✓ In his book *Who Is the Allah of Islam?* author Abd-al-Masih gives the Muslim view that Allah is "unique, unexplorable, and inexplicable." He flatly states that "Allah cannot be comprehended."

> ✓ Similarly, George Houssney writes in *What Is Allah Like?* that humans can never know Allah. They may know about him, but they do not have personal, experiential knowledge of him.

Muslims take offense at the notion that a person can know God. To the Islamic mind, a human ability to know God would make God dependent upon His creation. For this reason, Allah doesn't reveal himself; he reveals his *mashi'at* (desires and wishes), but not himself. Since Muslims believe that people cannot know Allah, they don't try to.

Muslims reject the Christian concept that God is immanent (meaning that His presence and activity are within the world and human nature, and that characteristics of God can be seen in the world around us). Muslims are also offended by the Christian concept that humans can establish a personal relationship with God. For the Muslim, Allah remains mysterious, distant, and unapproachable.

• *No Sacred Schizophrenia*

Perhaps the greatest difference between the Muslim's and the Christian's concept of God involves the concept of the Trinity. Muslims believe in the unity of Allah, meaning that he could have no son or partner. Many Muslims mistakenly believe that Christians worship three gods (which would be *tritheism*). However, this assumption comes from a misunderstanding of the Christian doctrine of the Trinity, which recognizes that there is only *one* God, but that there are three coexisting "Persons" within a unity of God: God the Father, Jesus the Son, and the Holy Spirit.

There is no Arabic word for "three-in-one" or "threefold," so it may be understandable that a language difficulty creates some misunderstanding of the Trinity. But Islam's rejection of the Trinity is much more than just a linguistical hurdle. The Qur'an specifically attacks the concept. In his book *The Koran Interpreted*, A.J. Arberry says that the Qur'an emphasizes that Christians are unbelievers because they accept the historic Christian doctrine of the Trinity. He quotes the Qur'an as saying, "They are unbelievers who say, 'God is the Third of Three.' No god is there but one God."

Doctrine #2: Angels

Muslims believe in a hierarchy of created beings. At the lowest level would be the animals, above them are the humans, and angels are an intermediate step between humanity and Allah.

There are good angels and bad angels. The good angels are the messengers of Allah, and the top one of highest rank is Gabriel (the one who gave the revelations of Allah to Muhammad in the cave). *Shaitan* is the fallen angel, and his fellow bad angels are called *jinns* (demons).

Each human being has two recording angels who keep track of all of the good deeds and bad deeds that a person does during his or her life. These angels play an important role on Judgment Day when they tell who has been naughty or nice.

Doctrine #3: Sacred Scriptures

Muslims are known as "people of the book," so it is not surprising that they regard certain writings as holy. According to Islam, Allah has revealed himself through four sacred writings:

- The Torah (the books of Moses in the Bible)
- The Zabur (the Psalms of David)

- The Injil (the gospel of Jesus Christ)
- The Qur'an (the revelations that Muhammad recited to his transcribers)

Because the Qur'an was the final message of Allah to his people, it supersedes all previous revelations. If there is any conflict among the writings, then the Qur'an prevails.

Dr. George Braswell, a scholar in the field of world religions, wrote this about the Qur'an:

> Of the scriptures of all the religions of the world, perhaps the Qur'an is looked upon by its followers as ideally and practically the most holy. Muslims believe that the Qur'an was revealed to the prophet, Muhammad, in the Arabic language, which is the very language spoken by Allah in heaven. Allah is the author of the Qur'an, and Muhammad is the channel of Allah's word to the people.

The Qur'an includes a lot of information that was already included in the Bible. More than 20 prophets—including Abraham, Moses, and Jesus—are mentioned. Much of the teaching about God in the Qur'an is consistent with the Bible, such as the belief that God is sovereign. The Qur'an also contains a number of stories that are similar to events from the Jewish and Christian traditions. Islam accepts the Jewish Torah and the Christian gospels (the Injil) as Allah's revelation to the pre-Islamic people.

However, Islam teaches that the Torah and the Injil were "misinterpreted" by Jews and Christians. In effect, those writings were corrupted. In contrast, the Qur'an is believed to be preserved in

Dr. Hazen Adds...

*T*here is another key difference between Islam and Christianity: the way in which they approach their holy books. In Islam, the Qur'an is considered the perfect word of Allah right from the beginning of the discussion. Hence, the Qur'an can never be called into question on statements it makes about facts or historical events. This is an example of circular reasoning. Evangelical Christian scholars, on the other hand, don't start out with the assumption that the New Testament is the word of God, but rather first show that it is a reliable historical account about Jesus and then work from there to show that it is divinely inspired.

its original perfect state. The entire text of the Qur'an was not completed until after Muhammad's death (because there was always the possibility that fresh revelations could be added while he was still alive). However, when the prophet died, his followers decided to make a collection of the whole Qur'an into a single book. Here is how it was accomplished:

- Islamic tradition holds that many of Muhammad's disciples, including four men closest to him, knew the Qur'an in its entirety during Muhammad's lifetime. A problem arose when a number of Islamic tribes in the Arabian Peninsula reverted to paganism after Muham-mad's death. They revolted against Muslim rule, so Abu Bakr, Muhammad's chief successor, sent an army to subdue the rebels. In the ensuing battles, many of the disciples who knew the Qur'an directly from Muhammad were killed.

- Abu Bakr realized that there was a danger that the Qur'an might be lost if any more of its most trusted reciters died, so he commissioned Zaid ibn Thabit to search for all existing portions of the Qur'an and collect them into a single book. It was a difficult task, because the contents of the Qur'an were widely scattered. There were many followers who had memorized parts of Muhammad's revelations, and selected portions had been written down on a variety of materials. Zaid had an assembly project that involved bits of pieces (from writings and memories).

- Zaid wasn't the only one who was working to collect the pieces and recollections of the Qur'an into a single text. There were others who claimed to have learned as many

Dr. Hazen Adds...

*R*ecent archaeological digs and manuscript finds have called into question much of the traditional story of the origins of Islam and the Qur'an. For instance, the prayer stones in the earliest mosques point toward Jerusalem and not Mecca. Also, the evidence is increasingly clear that Mecca was not a viable city in Muhammad's day and was not even on the Arab trade routes. New early manuscript finds indicate key differences between the earliest copies of the Qur'an and the ones in use today.

Other Books on the Islamic Shelf

Although the Qur'an is the final and ultimate authority for all Muslims, there are other important "written traditions" that serve as guides in faith and practice:

- Sunnah are sayings of Muhammad that show how he acted while leading his followers. The Sunnah were collected by Muslim scholars into a book called the *Hadith*.

- The *Qiyas* is an agreement of a Muslim community on interpretations of the Qur'an and the Hadith.

- The *Shari'ah* is a conduct guide for Muslims.

as 70 surahs (chapters) directly from Muhammad, but Islamic tradition pays special attention to Zaid's work, even though it differs from other collections.

Muslims claim that the present-day Qur'an is an exact representation of Muhammad's revelations without so much as a dot or stroke ever having been lost, changed, or substituted in any way.

Doctrine #4: Prophets

Like Christianity and Judaism, Islam is a prophetic religion. Muslims believe that over 100,000 prophets have been sent to human beings throughout history. The Qur'an names the more important ones (which number fewer than 30). You might recognize some of the names:

- Adam
- Noah
- Abraham
- Moses
- David
- Solomon
- Jonah
- John the Baptist
- Jesus

While Jesus is recognized as an important prophet in Islam, He isn't viewed as the Son of God. It is blasphemy to a Muslim to suggest that Jesus could be God, and the Qur'an emphatically denies it. Interestingly, however, Muslims believe that Jesus Christ was sinless. (Not even Muhammad shares this distinction.) And the Qur'an even teaches that Jesus was born of a virgin. But Muslims deny that Christ's distinctives (such as His perfection and virgin birth) are evidence that He was God in human form. They respect and honor Jesus, but they consider Him to be of less significance than Muhammad.

Each prophet brought a particular truth from Allah that was needed for that particular time. Muhammad, however, was the greatest prophet, and the message that he brought applies to everyone for all time.

Doctrine #5: Future Judgment

Muslims (like Jews and Christians) don't believe that physical death is the end of life. They believe that life includes a spiritual dimension that continues after death. (We guess that is why it is referred to as the afterlife.) Everyone who has ever lived will be resurrected from the dead at some unknown future time. When that happens, it will be time for the great Day of Judgment.

The Qur'an teaches that all human activities are written down by two angels. At the time of judgment, these two angels review the database on each individual. The actions of each person are weighed on a scale of absolute justice by Allah. The good deeds are balanced against the evil deeds. The way the scale tips (to the "good" side or to the "bad" side) determines the person's eternal

Looking for a Loophole

There is one loophole that would allow a Muslim— and only a Muslim—to avoid judgment. Those who die as martyrs in defense of the Islamic faith or in a "holy war" (a *jihad*) go directly to heaven and avoid the uncertain outcome of waiting to see which way the scales tip.

destiny. If your good deeds outweigh your bad ones, you go to heaven; if your bad deeds are heavier, then you'll be spending eternity in a place of unimaginable suffering.

Leaning on the Five Pillars

Since hell is really miserable, and since eternity is a really long time, tipping the judgment scale in favor of good deeds becomes very important. But you don't get credit for your random acts of kindness (like tossing a quarter into a street musician's guitar case or saying *gesundheit* when someone sneezes). The only good deeds that qualify for the judgment scale are those that are compatible with the teachings of the Qur'an and the Hadith. Chief among those are the Five Pillars of Faith that each Muslim must perform if the scale is going to tip in his or her favor.

Pillar #1: Recite the Creed

It is called the *Shahadah* (which literally means "to bear witness"), and every Muslim is expected to publicly recite it. Its English translation says, "There is no God but Allah, and Muhammad is his messenger." This statement succinctly acknowledges the Muslim's belief in God's unique oneness, eternity, and sovereignty, and it also acknowledges that Muhammad is the top prophet. Repeating this phrase (in Arabic) throughout his lifetime confirms a person's membership in the Islamic faith.

Pillar #2: Pray the Prayers

Prayer is the discipline most consistent Muslims practice because it shows obedience to Allah. Prayer is a ritual carried out five times a day: at dawn, noon, mid-afternoon, after sunset, and at night. Prayers, which must be said facing the holy city of Mecca in Saudi Arabia, can be done at home or in the mosque or any convenient place, except on Fridays. On that day, Muslims must attend the mosque at noon to say their prayers together.

Pillar #3: Give the Alms

You've probably heard the expression "giving alms for the poor." Well, this is one of the five requirements of a practicing Muslim. Alms *(zakat)* equal 2.5 percent of a person's income. The money is given to the Muslim community to benefit widows, orphans, the sick, and travelers. Alms are also used for the institutional and administrative purposes of Islam (such as the building of mosques or the salaries of Muslim missionaries).

Pillar #4: Start the Fast

Fasting can be done for reasons of piety or penance; either way, Muslims observe an entire month of fasting during Ramadan (the ninth month of the Muslim lunar year—the same month that Muhammad first received the revelation of the Qur'an). Fasting is serious business, as Muslims abstain from food, drink, and pleasures from sunrise to sunset each day during the month; any eating must be accomplished after sunset and before dawn.

Pillar #5: Make the Pilgrimage

Every Muslim dreams of making a pilgrimage *(hajj)* to Mecca. This is not just a fantasy trip; the Qur'an requires it at least once in a lifetime (although there are a few limited exceptions for the sick or those who can't afford it). Each year, millions of faithful

---

Dr. Hazen Adds...

*I*t was the advent of the jumbo jet that really made the *hajj* a global unifying force in Islam. Muslims from Jakarta to Detroit can now make the sacred pilgrimage to Mecca without committing to months of expensive and dangerous travel. You could imagine that making the *hajj* would be a very different experience for a faithful Muslim in, say, fourteenth-century Beijing (and they were there at that time!).

Muslims descend on Mecca during the twelfth month of the Islamic calendar year to accomplish the prescribed rituals of the pilgrimage, which include praying vows and circling the Kaaba. To Muslims, the hajj is symbolic of the global unity of Islam and represents everyone's equality before Allah.

The Sunni–Shi'ite Split

There are a variety of sects (or divisions) within Islam, each with a slightly different slant on some doctrinal point of view. The two

What's the Kaaba?

Located within the center of the arena in the grand mosque, the Kaaba is a cube-shaped structure, about the size of a small building. It is draped in black cloth. Its far eastern corner contains a holy Black Stone. This is the most sacred place on earth for Muslims (and from wherever they stand about the globe, they face the Kaaba when they say their daily prayers).

There are certain traditions about the Kaaba: Adam (of "Adam and Eve" fame) is said to have laid the foundation; the Black Stone is where Abraham was tempted to sacrifice his son, Ishmael (not Isaac, as Jews and Christians believe); hundreds of prophets are buried in the area that surrounds its perimeter. While it had been a polytheistic shrine containing the statues of many gods, Muhammad cleansed the Kaaba in 630 and purified it for all time for the sake of Allah.

When a Muslim man visits the Kaaba, he puts on two seamless white sheets to symbolize equality of all before God. Women wear their ordinary clothes, which cover them from head to ankles.

primary and largest sects are the Sunnis and the Shi'ites. Looking at their differences will give you a better understanding of why the faith of some Muslims seems to be more political than that of others.

The split between the Sunnis and the Shi'ites dates back to the years not long after Muhammad's unexpected death in 632. He had not appointed a successor, and therein lies the basis for the primary disagreement.

- *The Shi'ites:* The Shi'ites broke away from mainstream Islam primarily over the issue of leadership. They believed that the successor of Muhammad should be in Muhammad's

The Beliefs of Islam

What About...	According to Islam...
God	He is the powerful ruler of the universe. Justice is his most important feature. The "oneness" of his character prohibits the Christian notion of a Trinity or the divinity of Christ. The presence of God is not revealed through supernatural signs but through the order of nature and the miracle of the Qur'an.
Humanity	Humans are in charge of creation under the authority of God. Their charge is to instill moral order in the world through the teachings of Islam. Each person is given a divine spark that enables him or her to perceive the truth and act on it. Thus, conscience is a higher value than love.
Sin	Each person is responsible for his evil deeds. These are tracked throughout one's lifetime by the recording angels. The human tendency toward sin comes from a weakness rather than from a sin nature.
Salvation and the Afterlife	Salvation depends upon a person's actions and attitudes during life. Thus, salvation is each person's own responsibility. You won't know your eternal destiny until the Day of Judgment, when the scale weighs your good deeds against your bad deeds and determines whether you will enter the worldly delights of heaven or be sentenced to the torments of hell.
Morals	Moral behavior is outlined in the teachings of the Qur'an and is seen in the acts of Muhammad (as recorded in the Hadith). For this reason, the Qur'an is perhaps the most memorized book in the world.
Worship	True worship of Allah is best revealed by strict adherence to the procedures of the Five Pillars.
Jesus	Born of a virgin and sinless in His life, Jesus was a great prophet, but certainly not God. Muhammad, also a mere mortal, was the greatest prophet.

bloodline. They also take the position that Islamic religious leaders should also be political leaders. This sect is the smaller of the two, and it predominates in countries such as Iran, Iraq, Lebanon, and parts of Africa.

- *Sunnis:* The Sunnis are known as "followers of the tradition" or "followers of the path." They believe that the leaders of Islam should be elected and that there should be a separation between the realms of religion and government. Sunnis comprise approximately 80 percent of the Muslim population and have the greater representation in the countries of Egypt, Saudi Arabia, and Pakistan.

What's That Again?

1. Islam is a monotheistic religion begun by the prophet Muhammad, who received revelations directly from Allah beginning in A.D. 610.

2. Allah is the Supreme Ruler of the universe. He is most often characterized in terms of judgment and power. Allah is impersonal and mysterious. It is impossible to know him.

3. The Qur'an was compiled by various reciters and transcribers. It is an infallible book (without error). While the Bible is also recognized as an important book, it is considered to have been corrupted. The Qur'an represents the last and final revelations of Allah and is authoritative in all discrepancies with other sacred writings.

4. The Muslim view of salvation involves works as well as faith. Of primary importance is the faithful performance of the rituals of the Five Pillars (the creed, prayers, alms, fasting, and pilgrimage).

5. Each person's eternal destiny is determined on the Day of Judgment by a scale that balances good deeds against bad ones. You cannot know during your lifetime whether you have done enough to ensure that the scale tips in favor of your good works.

Dig Deeper

If you are looking for a much more technical book (that is still fairly easy to follow), try *Understanding World Religions* by George W. Braswell, Jr. He takes an objective view of all religions, including Islam.

In her book *Islam: A Short History*, Karen Armstrong does a good job of discouraging the overly simplistic belief of the Western world that Islam is just an extreme religion that promotes authoritative government, female oppression, and terrorism.

The Origins of the Koran, edited by Ibn Warraq, contains some classic essays written over the last 150 years on Islam's holy book.

■ ■ ■

*Q*uestions for *R*eflection and *D*iscussion

1. What preconceptions did you have about Islam before reading this chapter? How have your views of Islam changed?

2. Given the culture surrounding Muhammad, why were his ideas about God offensive?

3. Compare the methods Muhammad used to gain converts with the methods Jesus used.

4. List three differences between the God of Islam and the God of Christianity.

5. What is the main difference in the way Muslims view the Qur'an and the way Christians view the Bible?

6. Why is it a problem for Islam that there are key differences between the earliest copies of the Qur'an and the ones in use today?

7. Can you understand why a devoted Muslim would be so careful to observe the five pillars of Islam? What are the advantages of a religion that requires its adherents to follow strict guidelines? What are the disadvantages?

■ ■ ■

Moving On . . .

Assuming that you began at page 1 and have read continuously to this point, you've now covered the world's three major monotheistic religions. That qualifies you to move to part 2, in which we summarize several major beliefs that take some fundamental principles from these monotheistic religions but add a few interesting twists. Don't worry about remembering everything you learned in the first three chapters; we'll remind you of the important stuff. But don't think for a moment that your time in chapters 1 through 3 was wasted. You've got a great foundation for being able to spot how the religions in part 2 change and tweak things a bit. You'll need to rely on that foundation because the differences can be subtle, even though they are significant.

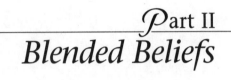

*P*art II
Blended Beliefs

*I*ntroduction to Part II

In part 2 we are going to look at several religions that we call "blended beliefs." By that we mean that these religions take some principles from Christianity and then *blend in* some of their own beliefs that are distinct and divergent from traditional Christian doctrine.

It's Time for a Sects Talk

Don't make the mistake of thinking that the blended beliefs that we will be talking about in chapters 4 through 6 are simply sects of Christianity. They aren't. The English word *sect* comes from the Latin word *sequi*. It means "to follow." Within the context of a major religion, a sect is a smaller group that adheres to a particular position on a point of doctrine. Webster defines a *sect* as "a faction of a larger group that follows a common leadership and a set of doctrines." The key to the definition of a sect is the fact that it remains within the larger group.

If you read part 1, you are already familiar with sect terminology. Christianity has its sects (usually referred to as "denominations"), such as Baptist, Methodist, and Presbyterian. The sects of Judaism include Orthodox, Reform, and Conservative. Within Islam, the Sunnis and the Shi'ites are the major sects.

In each of these religions, the members of the different sects acknowledge that they are all part of the same religion, despite their differences on a few doctrinal points or their denominational distinctions.

Within mainline Christianity, however, there is no such acknowledgment that the "blended beliefs" are part of the same religion. The doctrinal differences are too far apart on too many major points. Thus, the beliefs of chapters 4 through 6 aren't considered sects of Christianity. Instead, they are considered to be cults.

Is "Cult" a Four-Letter Word?

The common usage of the word *cult* usually has a negative connotation. Perhaps it brings to your mind an image of a dynamic leader who exercises control over a band of mindless followers and indoctrinates them with extremist views. You might be thinking of Jim Jones and the mass suicide of 913 members of the People's Temple in Jonestown, Guyana, back in 1978. Or, maybe the word *cult* causes you to recall David Koresh and the 82 members of the Branch Davidians who died at their compound in Waco, Texas, after a 51-day standoff with federal agents deteriorated into armed conflict and conflagration. While those are two examples of cults, they are at the extreme end of the definition. The blended beliefs that we'll be talking about in chapters 4 through 6 are on the other end.

The word *cult* comes from the Latin word *cultus*. Its original definition referred to members of an organization who cared about the same things. (The English word *culture* is derived from the same Latin word.)

When used in a religious context, the word *cult* defines a group that holds certain ideas and practices in common, but the specifics of its beliefs are either so new or so different that they take it way beyond the religion from which it started.

Theologians Dr. R.C. Sproul and Tim Couch have identified ten characteristics that typically distinguish groups that fit into the category of a cult. Here is their list (with our user-friendly explanations):

1. *An abrupt break with historic Christianity and its confessions.* Cults usually view historical Christianity as being off base for all of those centuries since Christ until their founder came along.

2. *Autosotericism.* This is theologian lingo for "self-salvation." Cults usually specify that salvation is obtained by following certain rules and regulations—those that are specified by the cult.

3. *A deficient Christology.* Christianity is premised on the belief that Jesus is God; if He is something less than God, then salvation by His death on the cross wouldn't work. Cults, however, take a lesser view of Christ. They might admire Him and view Him as greater than a human, but they don't consider Him as the one true God.

4. *Syncretism.* This is more theologian jargon that simply means the blending of different elements from several religions into one synthesized belief system.

5. *An emphasis on their own distinctives.* Rather than stressing the major doctrinal points of Christianity, a cult will put disproportionate emphasis on its distinguishing doctrines. Those things that mainline Christianity considers to be essential take a backseat to the cult's unique characteristics.

6. *Perfectionism.* Most cults teach that it is possible for a human to be perfect (a doctrine that flies in the face of Christianity's view that humans are sinful and can never achieve God's standard of perfection). Moral perfection is usually attainable by following the cult's prescribed conduct (doing some things and abstaining from others) and by adhering to the teachings of the cult's founder and leaders.

7. *An extrabiblical source of authority.* While many cults recognize the Bible as a sacred piece of literature, they have additional holy books. These other writings usually take precedence over the Bible (or they at least give the authoritative interpretation of the Bible). If there is a conflict between the two, the Bible comes in second place.

8. *A belief in exclusive community salvation.* A cult teaches that it is the only true church. Unless you believe all of its teachings, you won't be saved. In contrast, a *sect* of traditional Christianity won't claim exclusive rights to salvation; most denominational

differences don't pertain to the qualifications for salvation. According to the prevailing Christian viewpoint, joining a particular denomination is not a prerequisite to get to heaven. For most cults, however, you won't make it unless you are one of their members.

9. *A preoccupation with eschatology.* Eschatology is the study of the end of the world (or "the end times," as Christians like to call it). In the perspective of the time line of Christianity, most cults are brand-new (having been founded after Christianity had been rolling along 1800 years or so). Cults often explain that their founder brought the last word from God to prepare mankind for the end of the world. With this perspective, cults often emphasize urgency about the end of the world.

10. *Esotericism.* Something is esoteric if it is beyond the knowledge of most people and understood by only a select group of individuals. This is what separates cults from traditional Christianity. Each cult claims that its founder and/or leaders have access to special truth that was previously hidden.

A Distinguishing Difference

You might wonder why we didn't treat the blended beliefs of chapters 4 through 6 as offshoots of Christianity, or at least as other monotheistic religions. Why do they need to be segregated from part 1? After all, none of the religions in chapters 4 through 6 identify themselves as cults, so why should we?

While some of the religions discussed in the following chapters identify themselves as *Christian*, most followers of mainstream Christianity don't consider them to be such. It is the traditional Christian viewpoint that these blended beliefs are cults because they abandon or pervert fundamental doctrines of Christianity. In other words, they have been tweaked beyond recognition. Since adherents of historical Christianity view their religion as being irreconcilable with these alternative beliefs, we didn't feel we could lump them together.

We have categorized the religions of chapters 4 through 6 as a separate group because they qualify as *cults* according to the classical definition of that word. Not as radical as Jim Jones or David Koresh-type cults. Rather, as organizations that have developed a separate doctrine that is incompatible with the religion from which they trace their original roots.

Because of its negative connotation, repeated use of the *cult* label seems prejudicial. That's why we prefer "blended beliefs" or "blended-belief cults." Whatever the designation, however, you should realize that these religions have significant and substantive differences with Christianity. We aren't suggesting that you consider these blended beliefs to be wrong or invalid simply because their doctrine disagrees with the principles of Christianity. But don't think that the differences are inconsequential, either, because they are not.

As with all of the religions discussed in this book, there are millions of people who sincerely and enthusiastically have faith in these beliefs. For that reason alone, each one of these beliefs deserves your investigation and evaluation.

Chapter 4

Our minds being now enlightened, we began to have the Scripture laid open to our understandings, and the true meaning and intention of the more mysterious passages revealed unto us in a manner which we could never attain to previously...

Joseph Smith

Some of the nicest people you'll ever meet are Mormons. If you have a Mormon family for neighbors, then you have probably noticed their devotion to family, their high morals, and their involvement in the community.

As impressive as all of this is, Mormons are more than people who love their kids, live morally upright lives, and join the PTA. They are devout followers of a belief system that is growing faster than any other cult in the world. And it's as close as your front door. It is estimated that three-fourths of all new Mormon converts once had a previous Christian experience or affiliation. In fact, many people (including many Mormons) see very little difference between Mormonism and Christianity. Are Mormons and Christians basically the same, or are there significant differences? That's what we're going to find out.

Mormonism:
The One True Church?

*B*y all measurements, Mormonism—also known as the Church of Jesus Christ of Latter-day Saints (LDS)—is the most successful blended-belief cult in the world. With membership said to top 11 million worldwide, it is the *largest*. With a reported 300,000 converts a year, it is the *fastest growing*. And with assets of somewhere between 25 and 30 billion dollars, the Mormon Church is also the *wealthiest*.

Mormons are known for their missionary commitment. From an early age, Mormon children are told that it is their duty to the Church to go on a two-year mission immediately after they graduate from high school. That's why you see young Mormon men bicycling in your neighborhood, and it's also why there are more than 50,000 Mormon missionaries serving in 200 countries around the world.

Mormons resist the label of *cult*, because the term effectively separates them from orthodox Christianity. Mormons consider themselves Christians, and they will tell you that they believe in the Bible, God, and Jesus Christ. By all outward appearances, Mormons do appear to be Christians (in fact, many Mormons live moral lives that put many Christians to shame), but their beliefs tell a much different story.

As we will see, Mormon beliefs and practices differ dramatically from Christianity in almost every area.

They may use the same terminology, but when you look at what Mormons really believe, the differences become apparent. In virtually every area of belief, the Mormon Church is unorthodox, which means it doesn't follow traditional Christian beliefs.

---

*M*ormonism is Christianity; Christianity is Mormonism....Mormons are true Christians.

> Bruce R. McConkie, Mormon apostle, in Mormon Doctrine

Before we get into what Mormons believe, let's look at how the whole thing got started.

A Brief History of the Mormon Church

The founder of the Mormon Church was Joseph Smith. Born in Vermont in 1805, young Joseph grew up in Palmyra in upstate New York. Like most boys, he had a vivid imagination. One of Joseph's favorite activities was hunting for buried treasure. He also was a spiritually sensitive person, and he was bothered by the conflict he saw between the various church denominations (such as Baptist, Presbyterian, and Methodist). One day in the spring of 1820, Joseph was praying in the woods near his home when he received a vision in which two "personages"— the Father and the Son—appeared to him. The personages told him that all of the churches and their beliefs were wrong. A new church was needed, and Joseph Smith was the one to start and lead it.

Rather than act on his vision, Smith got more involved in treasure hunting. He used "seer" stones, commonly known as "peep" stones, to aid him in his search. In those days, "peep stone gazing" was considered an occultic practice (it was illegal too) because the peeper

A Quick Look at Mormonism

- The Mormon Church was founded in 1830 by Joseph Smith.

- Brigham Young replaced Smith as prophet in 1844.

- There have been 15 prophets of the Mormon Church, including the latest, Gordon B. Hinckley.

- Worldwide membership is more than 11 million. Half of all Mormons live outside the United States.

- There are more than 50,000 Mormon missionaries in 200 countries.

- Each Mormon missionary baptizes an average of six people per year for an estimated total of 300,000 new baptisms (converts) per year.

- The major thrust of Mormon missions is within Christian denominations.

- Mormons are required to tithe ten percent of their income annually.

- The Mormon Church generates three million dollars in income each day through tithes alone.

- More than three million copies of the *Book of Mormon* are distributed each year.

would place the stone into a hat and then put his face completely into the hat, shutting out all light. The magic rocks would shine in the darkness and supposedly reveal the location of buried treasure.

Joseph Smith and Moroni

On September 21, 1823, Smith claims he asked for another vision. This is when the angel Moroni appeared and told him there was a book inscribed on gold plates (buried somewhere near his home) containing information about the "former inhabitants" of America, along with an account of the true gospel, which had been given to these ancient inhabitants by the "Savior."

Smith had to wait three years before Moroni told him where the gold plates were buried. When Moroni finally revealed the location, Smith dug up the treasure and began translating the "reformed Egyptian hieroglyphics" by using a seer stone (known as the "Urim" and "Thummim") he found buried with the gold plates. By 1830, with the financial aid of a wealthy farmer, Smith published his translation of the gold plates, which he called the *Book of Mormon*, and he founded the Mormon Church. He began gaining converts to his "one true church," and from 1831 to 1844 Smith established Mormon strongholds in Ohio, Missouri, and Illinois.

Dr. Hazen Adds...

*A*ccording to Joseph Smith, this original *Book of Mormon* language called "reformed Egyptian" was spoken and written by millions of inhabitants of the Americas, but to this point not a single piece of evidence has been found to authenticate Smith's claim.

Opposition and Tragedy

As the Mormon Church grew, so did the opposition. The state of Missouri was especially intolerant of Mormon beliefs, since Smith continued to receive revelations, which he wrote down and published in various books he called "inspired Scripture." Some Mormons were jailed and others were killed, but many moved to Nauvoo, Illinois. The little town boomed as Smith became the mayor and commander-in-chief of his own army. He also came up with new revelations about the Godhead, the origin and destiny of the human race, eternal progression, baptism of the dead, and polygamy.

In fact, it was the practice of polygamy (Smith had more than 30 wives) that caused outsiders to object to (and many Mormon converts to seriously question) this new belief system. A group of disgruntled Mormons published a newspaper that exposed the "gross immoralities" among Church members. Smith and his "city council" attempted to destroy the office where the newspaper was

Moroni, Mormon, and the Ancient Inhabitants

According to traditional Mormon teaching, the angel Moroni was the son of the prophet Mormon, who wrote a book about two ancient civilizations that inhabited the American continent. The first of these civilizations, known as the Jaredites, came to the Western Hemisphere around 2250 B.C., but they were destroyed because of "corruption." The other civilization came to America across the Pacific Ocean from Jerusalem around 600 B.C. They were righteous Jews who escaped before the Babylonians captured the nation of Israel and destroyed their capital city.

The *Book of Mormon*, written on the gold plates, is the historical record of these two civilizations. These Mormon scriptures say that the second civilization, which eventually split into the Nephite and Lamanite nations, built dozens of cities and waged large-scale warfare, culminating in a massive battle that took place near Joseph Smith's home in New York State. Interestingly, not one shred of archaeological evidence for these civilizations or their cities exists. And since the angel Moroni took the gold plates back to heaven, they are not available for inspection.

printed, and he was arrested for rioting and charged with treason and conspiracy. On June 27, 1844, a mob of 200 stormed the jail in Carthage, Illinois, where Smith was being held and killed him, but not before Smith was able to wound some of his attackers with a smuggled gun.

New Leadership

Brigham Young, a Mormon apostle, took over leadership of the church. Young is best known for leading the Mormon faithful across the Great Plains in 1847 to the Great Salt Lake in Utah, where he established Salt Lake City, "the new Zion." Here the Mormons could practice their beliefs, including polygamy, which Brigham Young not only formalized as a practice but also encouraged. Polygamy flourished until 1890, when Wilford Woodruff, the fourth president of the Mormon Church, had a new reported revelation from God that Mormons give up the practice. Not coincidentally, the United States government had threatened to confiscate the church's temples and property and deny Utah the opportunity for statehood if the polygamous practices continued.

Basic Beliefs

Joseph Smith founded the Mormon Church as the one true church because he believed all other churches were corrupt. In his mind, there was no true church except for the Church of Jesus Christ of Latter-day Saints. So it shouldn't be surprising that the basic Mormon beliefs are in conflict with the basic Christian beliefs. Or, to return to our definition of a cult, Mormon beliefs are unorthodox.

Mormons will say they are Christians, and the strategy of Mormonism recently has been to blend the LDS Church with mainstream Christianity. But in order to know what Mormonism is all about today, you need to know the foundational beliefs as written down by the founding prophet, Joseph Smith. These beliefs are found in the four "standard works" of Mormon scripture.

Mormon Scriptures

Mormons accept four "standard works" of scripture: the *Book of Mormon*, *Doctrines and Covenants*, the *Pearl of Great Price*, and the Bible. To be clear, Mormons believe in the Bible "insofar as it is translated correctly." What this means is that while Mormons accept the original Bible manuscripts as being accurate, they believe that the text was corrupted along the way. They also believe that God continues to give revelations, which opens the door for Joseph Smith's "inspired" scripture. Here is a rundown of the four standard works:

> • The *Book of Mormon.* Joseph Smith once called the *Book of Mormon* "the most correct book on earth." Critics point

out that even though Smith claimed he "translated" the *Book of Mormon* from the writings of ancient civilizations, there is undeniable evidence that thousands of words in the *Book of Mormon*—including entire chapters from the Book of Isaiah—have been taken directly from the King James Version of the Bible.

• **Doctrines and Covenants.** Not only did Joseph Smith call the *Book of Mormon* the most "correct" book on earth, but he also claimed it was the most "complete." Nonetheless, three years after writing the *Book of Mormon*, Smith wrote the *Book of Commandments.* Two years later he substantially revised this book and called it *Doctrines and Covenants.*

• **Pearl of Great Price.** This sacred Mormon book, also written by Joseph Smith, is a "translation" from various Egyptian artifacts he had acquired. *Pearl of Great Price* contains Smith's own "correct" translation of the Book of Moses and the Gospel of Matthew, along with the Articles of Faith. Non-Mormon scholars have determined that the artifacts Smith used were in fact the remnants of a common Egyptian funeral text.

• **The "Inspired" Version of the Bible.** Smith believed and taught that every translation of the Bible was corrupt, so he did his own "translation." This was a tall order for Smith since he did not know Hebrew or Greek (the original languages of the Old and New Testaments). What he did was make thousands of changes to the King James Version. The Mormon version of the Bible includes a passage in Genesis 50 that predicts the coming of Joseph Smith.

Dr. Hazen Adds...

*A*ctually, Smith and many other members of the church took a limited number of Hebrew lessons from a rabbi named Josiah Sexius in Kirtland, Ohio, in the winter of 1834. But it is doubtful that any of them learned it well enough to become proficient at original translation in such a short period of time.

The Nature of God

Another important belief in the Mormon Church (or any church for that matter) is the nature of God. Who is God and what is He like? We don't have room to describe in great detail what Mormons believe about God (if you want to know more, check out the books listed in the Dig Deeper section at the end of the chapter). What we will do is highlight two important Mormon beliefs about the nature of God.

- *Eternal progression.* In the Mormon belief system, God is not the eternal, self-existent, all-powerful God of the universe. God is nothing more than a man who became a god. God was created by another god who existed before the Father God, who rules the universe today (and that god was created by a god before him, ad infinitum). The current Father God was once a mortal man, but he "progressed" to become God. Ron Rhodes quotes Milton R. Hunter, a Mormon theologian: "God the Eternal Father was once a mortal man who passed through a school of earth life similar to that through which we are now passing. He became God—an exalted being—through obedience to the same eternal Gospel truths that we are given opportunity today to obey." This belief that God was once a man leads to the belief that God still has a physical body.

- *Polytheism.* This is perhaps the most basic difference between Mormonism and orthodox Christianity. Not only do Mormons believe that the present Father God is descended from an eternal progression of other gods, but they believe that any Mormon can become God too. So, in effect, there are at least as many gods now as there are Mormons who in the past obeyed the "eternal Gospel truths." All faithful Mormons now living can also become gods. This belief in polytheism means that Mormonism is not in the tradition of monotheistic religions.

Dr. Hazen Adds...

*O*ne of the most fascinating episodes in Mormon history is the finding, translating, losing, and finding again of the famous "Book of Abraham" that is contained in *Pearl of Great Price*. Joseph Smith purchased some Egyptian mummies along with some old-looking papyrus scrolls from a traveling show in 1835. He then began translating the scrolls by the "gift and power of God," and he claimed they were none other than documents written by Abraham himself over 4000 years ago. No one knew how to translate the ancient Egyptian language at the time, so no one could test Smith's abilities. Eventually the original scrolls were lost.

An episode that occurred in our own generation, though, offered a very rare opportunity to test Joseph Smith's purported translating abilities. In 1967 some of the original papyrus pieces used by Smith to "translate" the Book of Abraham surfaced in a New York City museum. In what must have been a heartbreaking discovery to many Mormons at the time, modern Egyptologists made a translation that showed the documents had nothing whatsoever to do with the biblical patriarch Abraham. Rather, as Bruce and Stan point out, the scrolls turned out to be the ordinary Egyptian funeral documents that you would expect to find with mummies.

The Person of Jesus

According to Mormon theology, after the current Father God was created, he grew up as a man on another planet and then became God. He then had sex with the Mother God and had "millions" of spirit children. The firstborn of these spirit children was Jesus, and the second-born was Lucifer. The Father God came up with a plan for the rest of his spirit children to populate and live on earth and be tested, only to return to him after death (this is why you'll hear Mormons sometimes refer to Jesus as the "elder brother").

Jesus was chosen to be the Savior, which ticked off Lucifer, so he rebelled. The armies of heaven defeated Lucifer and banished

*A*s man is, God once was; as God is, man may become.

Lorenzo Snow, fifth Mormon President and Prophet

Dr. Hazen Adds...

*M*ormons reject the Christian belief in the Trinity, that God is one God in three Persons (Father, Son, and Holy Spirit). Mormons believe that the Father God, Jesus, and the Holy Spirit are three separate beings.

him to earth, which in the meantime had been created by Jesus and other spirit children. The way Jesus was born on earth happened this way: The Father God had physical relations with Mary.

Jesus grew up, got married, and had several children (some Mormons believe that Jesus was a polygamist). He died on the cross, was resurrected with a new body, and returned to heaven, where he is waiting to take the place of the Father God, who will progress to even greater realms.

Humankind

Mormonism teaches that every person who has ever been born once existed as a spirit in heaven (this is called "preexistence"). When you are born, you are basically following the pattern of Father God and Jesus. By becoming a Mormon and obeying Mormon

Dr. Hazen Adds...

*A*lthough it is still taught widely in the LDS church, the idea that the Father God had physical relations with Mary to produce Jesus is denounced in the School of Religious Education at Brigham Young University.

teaching, you can progress toward godhood (if you get married in a Mormon temple, you get your own planet). Once you have become a god, you can have spirit children of your own, and they will eventually come to earth and repeat the cycle.

- *Sin and salvation.* Because all people were once spirit children, they are born in an innocent state. Sin is not a condition of rebellion against God. It's more like having poor judgment or making a mistake. In Mormon theology, salvation is not how you get right with God. It simply means that you will be resurrected and have a body. Mormons believe that because Jesus (our elder brother) was resurrected, everyone will be resurrected. But you aren't saved by believing in Jesus and accepting Him as your Savior. All people are saved eventually, and you are saved individually by doing good works and by obeying "the laws of the Gospel," meaning people are saved by following the beliefs of the LDS Church.

• *The afterlife.* Joseph Smith taught—and Mormons believe—that when they die, all people will enter one of three heavens: the *celestial*, the *terrestrial*, or the *telestial*. Only faithful Mormons will enter the celestial heaven, which is the best one. The terrestrial heaven is second-best. This is where really good non-Mormons and not-so-good Mormons go. The third level, the telestial heaven, is for those people who have been mostly bad—and that includes most people.

Dr. Hazen Adds...

*T*here is a growing movement among some in the LDS church that embraces the traditional Protestant concept of salvation by grace alone without works. But it is not yet a dominant teaching.

Responding to Mormonism

In the opening pages of this book, we made it clear that our goal is not to convert or coax you into our belief system by making Christianity look good and all of the other religions and belief systems look bad. We simply want to present what other people believe as objectively as possible so that you can make your own decision. The only way to make a reasonable choice is to evaluate the options objectively.

When it comes to Mormonism (or any blended-belief cult, for that matter), we have to take another step. We can't discuss LDS beliefs without making some comparisons to Christianity. There are two reasons for this: 1) Mormons present their belief system as the one true version of Christianity, which they say is corrupt; and 2) Mormons use the same terminology as Christians but with different definitions.

So while it may seem that we are trying to make LDS beliefs look bad by comparing them to Christian beliefs, we are merely trying to be fair, both to Mormons and also to Christians. The only way to make an honest evaluation of anything is to know the terminology and what it means. If the definitions of the same word are *different*, then you need to find out which one is *true*. With that in mind, let's make a comparison of the definitions of three critical areas of belief where Mormons and Christians differ dramatically: *Scripture, God,* and *Jesus Christ*. Once we've done this, it's up to you to make the call.

The Authority of Scripture

When you consider any book of scripture from any belief system, it's important to evaluate the authenticity and reliability of that book, because this will tell you if it speaks with authority. If the followers of the belief system say their scripture came from God, then the followers need to find out how that happened. How did God write the scripture, and how did it come from Him to us?

Mormons claim that their four "standard works" of scripture have the authority of God. Let's take a look at the *Book of Mormon* (the most important of the four standard works) and the Bible and review how they got from God to us.

The Book of Mormon

- Joseph Smith translated the *Book of Mormon* from the writings of ancient prophets engraved on gold plates he found buried near his home.

- The translation involved a "seer stone," which Smith claimed gave him the power of God.

- The *Book of Mormon* contains thousands of words— including entire chapters—from the King James Version of the Bible.

- There is no decisive archaeological evidence for any of the ancient civilizations described by the *Book of Mormon*.

- Despite Mormon claims, the *Book of Mormon* is not prophesied in the Bible.

The Bible

- God used the Holy Spirit to *inspire* (literally, "breathe into") 40 different human writers (called *prophets*) over a period of 1600 years (2 Peter 1:20-21).

- Several different individual church councils discovered which writings were Scripture by recognizing the writings that spoke with the authority of God.

- The Bible has been carefully transmitted and translated from the original manuscripts and languages to the current day.

- Archaeologists have uncovered more copies of ancient Bible manuscripts than any other document of antiquity.

- There is abundant corroborating evidence to confirm the claims of the Bible. Not every person, place, date, or fact in the Bible has been verified by outside sources, but many have, and not one has been shown to be false.

Besides this comparison, you need to answer this question: If God was responsible for both the *Book of Mormon* and the Bible, wouldn't you expect these to agree with each other? In fact, there are many contradictions between the Mormon scriptures and the Bible. Because God is incapable of contradiction or deception (Hebrews 6:18), God could not have written them both.

The Nature of God

Let's review what the Mormon scriptures and prophets have taught about God:

- God the Father is an exalted man from another planet.

- He came from another species of gods, who existed before him in an infinite series of gods, who were also men.

- God is ever evolving.

- God has a physical body.

- God the Father had physical relations with the Mother God, resulting in millions of spirit babies.

- Although matter is eternal, God is not.

These qualities paint a picture of a god who is finite, changeable, limited, and one of many. In other words, God is pretty much like us (which is the whole point). Here's what the Bible, God's own written Word, says about God:

- God is God, not an exalted man (Hosea 11:9).

- There is only one God (Isaiah 45:5).

- God is a spirit (John 4:24) and does not have flesh and bones (Luke 24:39).

- God is eternal (Isaiah 40:28).

- God does not change (Malachi 3:6).

- There has never been a time when God was not completely God (Psalm 90:2).

These qualities present a God who is eternal, unchanging, and unique. And here's something else to consider. The God of the Bible is *transcendent*. That means He is independent of the universe itself. If God created the universe and all matter, then He couldn't have been a part of it. God had to exist before everything else existed (Psalm 90:2), which means He is self-existent. That means nobody created Him. God is the first cause and Creator of all things.

Science and philosophy agree that in order for the universe to exist, there must be a first cause or an intelligent designer that itself has no cause. Only the God of the Bible fits this description.

The Person of Jesus

Christianity would not exist without Jesus Christ. Mormonism treats Jesus as just another man who made good on earth. Essentially, here's what Mormons believe about Jesus:

- He was a created being and the brother of Lucifer.

- He was born as a result of Mary having physical relations with God.

- Jesus had to earn his own salvation, just like the rest of the created beings.

- Jesus is a "greater" being than other spirit children on the earth, but he has the same nature.

- Jesus was a polygamist.

- The atonement of Jesus took place in the Garden of Gethsemane and was for Adam's sin only.

- Our salvation begins with the atonement but is made complete by our good works.

The Bible gives a dramatically different description of Jesus and His work:

- Jesus is fully God and one with God the Father (John 10:30).

- Jesus was born of a virgin through the Holy Spirit (Matthew 1:18-20).

- Because He is God, Jesus didn't need to be saved (1 John 5:20).

- There is no evidence that Jesus ever married once, let alone several times.

- The atonement of Jesus took place on the cross, and it was effective for all humankind (Romans 5:18).

- There is no other way to be saved except by faith in Jesus Christ (Acts 4:12; Ephesians 2:8-9).

More than a Feeling

Oftentimes when confronted with the truth and teaching of the Bible regarding God, Jesus, and salvation, Mormons will become very subjective. They will say that the ultimate test for truth is an "inner feeling" or a "burning in the bosom" that tells them that the LDS Church is the one true church, and Mormonism is the one true belief system.

It's fine to have feelings, but they should never be the final test for truth. Certainly God produces feelings through the Holy Spirit, but do you think He would ever prompt a person to believe things that contradict His very being and His written Word?

What's That Again?

1. Mormonism is the most successful cult in the world. It is the largest, the fastest-growing, and the wealthiest.

2. Even though Mormons would rather be called Christians than a cult, Mormon beliefs and practices differ from Christianity in almost every area.

3. Joseph Smith claimed to have received a revelation from God the Father and God the Son that all churches were corrupt.

4. Smith claimed that the angel Moroni appeared to him and revealed the location of two gold plates that contained an account of the true gospel.

5. The Mormon belief system is built upon the teachings of the books that Smith wrote as a result of his revelations.

6. Smith claimed that the *Book of Mormon* was the most correct and complete book on earth. Mormons believe the *Book of Mormon* is God's perfect revelation to the world, whereas all translations of the Bible are corrupt.

7. Mormons believe that God was once a man, and man can become God.

8. In the Mormon belief system, Jesus is not God but the first being of millions of spirit babies. Jesus and Lucifer are brothers.

9. All people will eventually be resurrected and will get into one of three heavens. Only Mormons who have faithfully followed the teaching of the Mormon Church will get into the top level of heaven.

10. Because the Mormon Church claims to be the one true church with the only true beliefs, it's important to evaluate the beliefs of Mormonism objectively.

Dig Deeper

One of the classic books on Mormonism and other cults is *The Kingdom of the Cults* by Dr. Walter Martin, who was an expert on comparative religion. His research and documentation are very thorough.

Dr. Hazen is a contributor to *The New Mormon Challenge,* an important book that shows how to repectfully engage the Mormon viewpoint.

Mormonism by Kurt Van Gorden quotes extensively from the Mormon standard works and documents, and then offers arguments to support biblical Christianity.

Two other excellent books suggested by Dr. Hazen are *Mormonism 101* by Bill McKeever and Eric Johnson, and *The Changing World of Mormonism* by Jerald and Sandra Tanner.

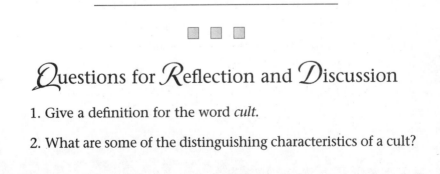

Questions for Reflection and Discussion

1. Give a definition for the word *cult.*

2. What are some of the distinguishing characteristics of a cult?

3. What do you think is the appeal for people to join the Church of Jesus Christ of Latter-day Saints?

4. Why do Mormons want to insist that their beliefs are "Christianity" when their principles have significant differences with traditional doctrines of the Christian faith?

5. If you were a Mormon, how would you defend skepticism about the gold plates and the seer stones that were used by Joseph Smith and never seen by any other individual?

6. What are the ramifications if there is not a single, pre-existent, all-powerful God of the universe, but rather a God who progressed from being a man?

7. Explain why it is important to define terminology if people of two faiths use similar doctrinal words that have different meanings.

Moving On . . .

You're going to find that the blended-belief cults in this section of the book differ in some of their beliefs. But when it comes to the reality of the Trinity and the divinity of Jesus, they are remarkably similar. Like Mormons, Jehovah's Witnesses deny the Trinity exists, and they teach that Jesus is a lesser god. To find out more, keep reading.

Chapter 5

Today, where it is possible, Jehovah's Witnesses endeavor to call at each home several times a year, seeking to converse with the householder for a few minutes on some local or world topic of interest or concern. A scripture or two may be offered for consideration, and if the householder shows interest, the Witness may arrange to call back at a convenient time for further discussion.

www.watchtower.org

Unless it is Girl Scout cookie season, that knock at your door on a Saturday morning is likely to be two of the Jehovah's Witnesses. Their zealous door-to-door evangelism has made them one of the fastest-growing religions.

In their extensive array of evangelistic printed material, the Jehovah's Witnesses identify themselves as Christians without highlighting their many significant departures from traditional biblical doctrine. Much of their promotional literature is generic in nature and emphasizes the importance of spiritual guidance for personal welfare, healthy marriages, and strong families. A more in-depth examination of their beliefs, however, reveals clear-cut and fundamental differences with mainstream Christianity.

The doctrinal positions of the Jehovah's Witnesses result in a lifestyle that puts them at odds with many political and social institutions and practices. The opposition they have experienced certainly hasn't deterred them. It seems to have strengthened their commitment to their faith.

Jehovah's Witnesses:
A View from the Watchtower

*W*hat's *A*head

- ☐ Knock, Knock! Who's There?
- ☐ The Mount Rushmore of Jehovah's Witnesses
- ☐ Witness This
- ☐ I'm Opposed to That

*A*s religions go, Jehovah's Witnesses are a late arrival to the party. (Actually, that is a poor analogy because they abstain from festivities and celebrations. But more about that later.) Their organization didn't begin until 1872. Even though they got a late start, they have achieved worldwide recognition and acceptance due to their aggressive evangelistic endeavors. If you think that the phenomenal growth of the Jehovah's Witnesses has been achieved through the technological advancements of the twentieth century, you are wrong. They have done it the old-fashioned way: walking through neighborhoods and knocking on one door at a time.

Knock, Knock! Who's There?

Jehovah's Witnesses are interested in their spiritual condition and yours. That's part of the motivation for their door-to-door evangelism efforts. As far as *your* spiritual welfare is concerned, knocking at your door is how they introduce you to their beliefs. As far as *their* spiritual condition is concerned, the door-to-door witnessing fulfills one of the most important requirements for their salvation.

On average, each Witness spends about ten hours each month engaged in these door-to-door visits. (Some of them do it on a full-time basis and log over 100 hours a month.) Detailed and precise statistics are kept on this universal witnessing effort. It has proven to be effective, as converts are gained at the rate of about 5500 per week.

A Quick Look at Jehovah's Witnesses

- The Jehovah's Witnesses movement was founded in the late 1800s by Charles T. Russell in Pittsburgh.

- There are currently over 6,000,000 Witnesses in 230 countries of the world.

- In the United States, there are approximately 988,000 Witnesses. That's about 1 out of every 277 residents.

- There are approximately 91,500 congregations worldwide, with about 11,500 of those in the United States.

- According to the Watchtower Bible and Tract Society, Jehovah's Witnesses held almost 425,000 Bible studies in the United States and more than 4,750,000 Bible studies worldwide in calendar year 2000.

- In that same year, there were about 181,500,000 hours of sermons given in the United States, and 1.1 billion hours of preaching throughout the world by Witnesses.

As you can imagine, these door-to-door missionaries meet with their share of rejection and challenges. But they are prepared for it. Each one of them is well-trained. Every Jehovah's Witness must attend five hours of meetings each week:

- There is a two-hour public meeting each Sunday that includes an analysis of an article from *The Watchtower* magazine.

- There is a one-hour meeting during the week (usually on Tuesday) when one of the other publications of the Watchtower Bible and Tract Society is studied.

- Another two-hour meeting is held (usually on Thursday) for the presentation of a lesson from the Bible or a Watchtower publication, as well as a demonstration on techniques for witnessing to non-Jehovah's Witnesses.

These meetings don't involve audience participation. No questions are allowed. According to an article in *The Watchtower*, questions could be viewed as arousing suspicion, so each member is instructed to accept the teachings of the Watchtower Society as authoritative, definitive, and final.

Who's in Charge?

In contrast with many Christian churches that are affiliated with a denomination yet have a high degree of autonomy, the Jehovah's Witnesses are a tightly organized religion. While Witnesses meet in a local "Kingdom Hall," strict guidelines on issues of structure and doctrine are dictated from the "Governing Body" at the global headquarters located in Brooklyn, New York. Here is how an official publication of the Jehovah's Witnesses outlines its structure:

- The Governing Body sends representatives each year to various regions worldwide to confer with the branch representatives in those regions.

- In these regional offices, there are Branch Committees of about three to seven members to oversee the work in the lands under their jurisdiction.

- The country or area served by each branch is divided into districts, and the districts, in turn, are divided into circuits. A district overseer visits the circuits in his district in rotation. Two assemblies are held annually for each circuit.

- Each circuit has in it about 20 congregations. A circuit overseer visits each congregation in his circuit usually twice a year, assisting the Witnesses in organizing and doing the preaching work in the territory assigned to that congregation.

- The Kingdom Hall is the gathering place for the local congregation. The geographic region for each Kingdom Hall is mapped out in small territories. These areas are assigned to individual Witnesses who endeavor to visit and speak with the people in every single home and apartment in their area.

- Each congregation, consisting of from a few to some 200 Witnesses, has elders assigned to look after various duties. Every one of the Witnesses, whether serving at the world headquarters, in branches, or in congregations, does this fieldwork of personally telling other people about God's kingdom.

A Whole Lot of Literature

We suspect that there aren't many environmentalists in the organization because the Jehovah's Witnesses must kill a lot of trees to provide the paper for their vast array of publications. The Watchtower Bible and Tract Society of Pennsylvania is the official publisher for the religion. Its publications include...

- *New World Translation of the Holy Scriptures:* This is the Bible, but in their own proprietary translation.
- *The Watchtower:* their primary magazine that is used for witnessing and doctrinal instruction. It is printed in 132 languages, with a print run of 22,000,000 copies per issue.
- *Awake:* another witnessing and doctrinal magazine published in more than 80 languages.
- Miscellaneous books, brochures, and study aids.

The Mount Rushmore of Jehovah's Witnesses

You could get a fairly good overview of American history by hearing the stories of the U.S. presidents who had their faces carved in stone on Mount Rushmore. There is no such monument for the presidents of the Jehovah's Witnesses, but the early history of the religion can be logically divided into three periods that coincide with the first three men who served as president.

Charles T. Russell

The Jehovah's Witness movement was founded by Charles T. Russell in Pittsburgh, Pennsylvania, in the late 1800s. In the decade before Russell's birth, there had been intense interest in the return of Christ, predicted by William Miller to occur in 1842. When 1842 came and went without Christ returning to establish His millennial (1000-year) kingdom, Miller adjusted his prediction to 1844. That prediction was also inaccurate and Miller was discredited, but some of his followers went on to form the Advent Christian Church (in 1860), and others formed the Seventh-day Adventists (in 1863).

As a child, Charles Russell grew up believing in the traditional notions of Christianity. As a young man, however, he became skeptical of the existence of a literal hell. In 1872, he was 20 years old and employed as a clerk at a men's clothing store. At that time he encountered members of a Seventh-day Adventists group and was intrigued by the notion of an imminent return of Christ to establish the millennial era. He established the International Bible Students' Association and predicted that the millennial age would begin in 1914. By 1881 his organization was known as Zion's Watchtower Tract Society, and he printed the first edition of the magazine now known as *The Watchtower*.

By 1888, 50 people were involved full-time in this upstart religious movement. Russell's skills as a communicator helped stimulate much of the interest. In addition to his published sermons, he penned a seven-volume series, Studies in the Scriptures, that became the doctrinal foundation for his followers (as he said that it would be better to read his writings than the Bible).

Russell's predictions for 1914 didn't happen like he had predicted. Although tumultuous events occurred at the outbreak of

World War I in 1914, Russell was later forced to adjust his prediction. Subsequent predictions were not fulfilled either. (Present-day Jehovah's Witnesses readily admit this, but they attach great significance to the fact that World War I began in 1914, which changed the course of history.)

Joseph Franklin "Judge" Rutherford

Charles Russell died in 1916. His successor was Joseph Rutherford. As the "new oracle of God's message for this age," Rutherford expanded the written literature by writing an average of one new book each year. Rutherford's writings became the new standard for doctrinal and scriptural reinterpretation. (To the extent that they were contradictory, Russell's writings and interpretations were dismissed as not consistent with the current progressive light.)

Rutherford instituted many significant changes affecting evangelistic efforts:

- He introduced another magazine called *The Golden Age* (now known as *Awake*).

- He reinforced the emphasis on door-to-door witnessing.

- Radio broadcasts were used extensively in the 1920s and 1930s. Under the auspices of the renamed Watchtower Bible and Tract Society, 403 radio stations were broadcasting Bible lectures in 1933. Later, radio broadcasts were phased out as Witnesses were equipped with portable phonographs and recorded Bible talks to use on their door-to-door visits.

- In 1931, to distinguish themselves from Christian denominations, the name of the group was changed to Jehovah's Witnesses.

What's in a Name?

Jehovah's Witnesses might seem a little awkward for the name of a religion, but it is descriptive of who these people are and what they believe. *Jehovah* is one of the Hebrew names for God recorded in the Old Testament. It is their mission to tell everyone in the world about God. Thus, they are Jehovah's witnesses.

Nathan H. Knorr

When Joseph Rutherford died in 1942, Nathan Knorr assumed the position of president of the Witnesses. This occurred during a time when many Witnesses were being arrested in connection with their religious opposition to political requirements (such as refusing to serve in the military, as discussed below). The Witnesses were involved in many court cases to preserve their freedom of speech, press, assembly, and worship. Between the 1930s and 1940s, they won 43 cases before the Supreme Court of the United States. In his book *These Also Believe,* Professor C.S. Braden said of the Witnesses, "They have performed a signal service to democracy by their fight to preserve their civil rights, for in their struggle they have done much to secure those rights for every minority group in America."

During Knorr's administration, a special training school for missionaries was established to facilitate worldwide missionary efforts. Under his leadership, the Witnesses grew from a total of 115,000 followers (in 1942) to more than two million members (in 1977).

Witness This

The Witnesses affirm that the Bible is their only authority, but they do not hold to conventional interpretations. They believe they alone interpret the Bible correctly, and they use their own version of the Bible (the New World Translation).

Because there is this similarity with a different twist, perhaps the distinctive beliefs of the Witnesses can best be presented by identifying some of the issues where there is outright disagreement with the traditional positions of Christianity. There are many such issues, but here are a few that are fundamental:

There Is God, but No Trinity

The Witnesses believe that there is one God—Jehovah. There is only one correct name for God—Jehovah. The Witnesses interpret the Bible to say that the exclusive use of the name *Jehovah* is a mark of the only true religion.

They don't consider Jesus to be the Son of God. Instead, Jesus is actually Michael the archangel, who was the first of God's creations. When Michael came to earth, then he was called Jesus. After the resurrection, when Jesus returned to heaven, he was back to being Michael the archangel.

Because Jesus isn't God, the Witnesses can't pray to him. It would be heresy to do so. Anyone found "guilty" of such a transgression is disassociated from the organization in disgrace.

They have a concept of the Holy Spirit, but not as God. Rather, the Holy Spirit is an active force (like electricity).

Dr. Hazen Adds...

The Witnesses spend a great deal of time attempting to show that a famous Bible passage, John 1:1, actually says that Jesus was "a god" in addition to the God named Jehovah. That makes the Witnesses polytheists by definition—but polytheism is something that they officially denounce.

There Is Life After Death (for the Witnesses), but No Hell (for Everyone Else)

Just as Charles Russell determined as a young man, the Witnesses deny the existence of hell. That means there is no eternal punishment. All non-Witnesses are annihilated immediately upon death—no prolonged pain or torture in an afterlife, just evaporation.

For the Witnesses, there is an afterlife. There will be an elite ruling class of 144,000 who actually get admitted to heaven. (Less than 9000 of them live on earth today.) The rest of the Witnesses will live on a new-and-improved earth, which Jehovah will establish in the millennium. Until then, the spirits of the faithful Witnesses who die will remain in an unconscious state until they are resurrected in the millennium.

There Is Salvation, but You Have to Work for It

Because Jesus (really Michael the archangel) is not considered to be God, he doesn't play a very significant role in the salvation process. His death on the cross cancels out Adam's sin. Since we don't have that sin nature hanging over our heads from our original ancestor, we have the chance to be righteous on our own. This happens by being a Witness and testifying for Jehovah.

The Beliefs of the Jehovah's Witnesses

What About...	According to Jehovah's Witnesses...
God	His personal name is Jehovah. He alone is God. There is no Trinity (which is a lie originated by Satan). There is a Holy Spirit, but it is just another name for God's active force.
Humanity	Humans are God's creation. Those who are faithful Jehovah's Witnesses have an eternal spirit. Non-Witnesses have no eternal nature after death (you just return to non-existence).
Sin	Sin is falling short of God's perfection. Adam and Eve sinned, and all humans inherit sin from them.
Salvation and the Afterlife	Adam deliberately forfeited the perfect life he was originally given. This was offset by Christ forfeiting His own perfect life. Christ's death didn't pay the penalty for sin, but it brought back the possibility for perfection in the human life. The 144,000 faithful followers of Jehovah will be rewarded with heaven; the rest of the faithful Witnesses will have everlasting life on a peaceful earth.
Morals	There is little subjectivity in this regard. Morality is for the most part defined by the prohibitions and requirements set forth in specific teachings.
Worship	True worship takes the form of adherence to certain requirements, particularly door-to-door evangelistic efforts. Reverence and allegiance to Jehovah prohibits participation in birthday parties and similar celebrations, displays of patriotism, and military service.
Jesus	He was God's first creation. His prehuman existence was as Michael the archangel. He was born of the virgin Mary, He died on a stake (not a cross) and was raised as an immortal spirit by God.

Consequently, salvation is not based on a relationship with Jesus Christ. Instead, it is based on faithfulness to the procedures and requirements of the institution of Jehovah's Witnesses.

I'm Opposed to That

Most religions are opposed to certain activities that would be considered immoral. It is usually a subjective standard, so ordinarily there isn't a benefit to listing the "do's and don'ts" of any religion. Jehovah's Witnesses, however, have gained notoriety for their refusal to participate in activities that no other religion finds objectionable. The Witnesses claim that their position is mandated by the Bible and that anyone who claims to believe the Bible must come to the same conclusion.

Based on their interpretation of the Bible, the Witnesses refrain from practices such as these:

- *Blood transfusions:* This position is based on verses in Leviticus and Acts dealing with blood from animal sacrifices. Any Witness who accepts a blood transfusion is "disfellowshipped" and ostracized by other Jehovah's Witnesses.

- *Birthday celebrations:* Birthday parties tend to give excessive importance to the individual. Such special recognition only belongs to Jehovah. Also, there were only two birthday celebrations mentioned in the Bible, and both involved pagans (and both involved someone's execution).

- *Christmas celebrations:* The real date of Jesus' birthday is unknown, and the date of December 25 coincides with a pagan holiday.

- *Other parties and festivities (such as Thanksgiving):* Jehovah is opposed to the excessive eating that often accompanies such celebrations.

- *Patriotic customs:* The Witnesses don't vote, and they don't salute the flag. They are citizens of Jehovah's kingdom, and they don't claim or owe allegiance to any other kingdom or nation.

- *Serving in the military:* The Witnesses are part of Jehovah's army. Any other military organization is the enemy. Consequently, as a matter of conscience, they do not participate in armed conflict or even in noncombative military duty.

What's That Again?

1. Jehovah's Witnesses are fervent in their efforts at door-to-door witnessing. They spend hours each week studying their beliefs so that they are prepared for this missionary endeavor. They are motivated by a concern for your spiritual condition and by the fact that this door-to-door witnessing is a requirement for their salvation.

2. The door-to-door evangelism has made Jehovah's Witnesses one of the fastest-growing religions.

3. Jehovah's Witnesses around the world are part of a highly structured religious organization under the auspices of the Watchtower Bible and Tract Society. The controlling literature is the Bible (only in the authorized New World Translation) and the doctrinal magazines such as *The Watchtower* and *Awake*.

4. The religion was founded in 1872 around the prediction of Charles Russell that Christ was going to return to earth and establish a millennial kingdom in 1914.

5. Although the Witnesses identify themselves as Christian, they reject many of the foundational Christian doctrines, such as the Trinity, the deity of Jesus, and salvation through Christ's death on the cross.

6. On the basis of reverence and allegiance to Jehovah, the Witnesses abstain from parties, patriotic expressions, and military service.

Dig Deeper

The official website for Jehovah's Witnesses is www.watch tower.org. This site is designed for promotional purposes to introduce people to the fundamentals of the religion.

The Harper Collins Dictionary of Religions is a thick, single-volume reference that provides a good review of all religions, including Jehovah's Witnesses. We found it useful for a quick, short overview to remind us of a few basics.

Sometimes the best way to understand a religion is to look at points of disagreement. In *How to Respond to Jehovah's Witnesses*, Herbert Kern suggests issues for discussion where there is a difference of opinion between traditional Christianity and Jehovah's Witnesses. We appreciate the fact that his suggestions are premised on a respect for each viewpoint.

◼ ◼ ◼

*Q*uestions for *R*eflection and *D*iscussion

1. Have you ever had a Jehovah's Witness knock at your door? What happened? What was your impression?

2. The New World Translation of the Holy Scriptures, magazines, and other printed matter are a key part of the Jehovah's Witnesses' strategy. Why do you think reading material plays such a big part? Why do think reading is essential to almost every religion and cult?

3. In what ways have Jehovah's Witnesses helped the cause of every religion in America, including Christianity?

4. The Witnesses claim to be the only ones who interpret the Bible correctly. Give three reasons why this is an impossible claim.

5. Show how the Witnesses are polytheists, even though polytheism is something they denounce.

6. Give two examples that show the Jehovah's Witnesses' belief system is based on works.

7. How is Jesus as revealed in the Bible different from Jesus as taught by Jehovah's Witnesses?

■ ■ ■

Moving On . . .

Remember that part 2 focuses on blended beliefs—those religions that take certain parts of Christianity and blend them with nontraditional doctrines and beliefs. Although both Mormonism and Jehovah's Witnesses have major conflicts with Christianity, there is some significant commonality, and it isn't too difficult to spot.

As we move into chapter 6, you'll have to look harder for the common connections. We are still dealing with blended beliefs that borrow some notions from traditional Christianity, but the differences will be getting more severe.

Chapter 6

May the Force be with you.

Yoda

The human race has always been very impressed with itself, and for good reason. Blessed with superior intelligence, the ability to reason, and an acute sense of self-awareness, we stand apart from and above every other creature that has ever slithered, crawled, or walked on the earth (and that includes lawyers). Oh, and we have one more very important thing going for us: We bear God's image.

But having all of these advantages hasn't helped us much, at least not when it comes to always doing the right thing. We seem to always be telling God, "Hey, You might be the Creator and all, but we can do this on our own." Other times we say to God, "We don't like the way You are, so we're going to recreate You in *our* image."

That's pretty much what the Mormons and Jehovah's Witnesses have done, but they're not the only ones. A bunch of other blended-belief cults have come out of this idea that we as a human race have all the brains we need to do things our own way. You may not have heard of all of these so-called mind sciences, but by the time this chapter is over, you're going to know exactly what they're thinking.

The Mind Sciences:
A New Way of Thinking

*S*tarting your own religion is kind of like baking a cake. Just as there are different kinds of cakes, there are different kinds of religions. Some are multilayered, some are light, some are rich, and some have nuts. But no matter how different they are, cakes and religions alike have to start with some basic ingredients. You know what goes into a cake: flour, salt, baking soda, butter, and eggs. Here are some directions for starting your own religion:

- Claim to have divine inspiration.
- Make God more like humans (or merely a force).
- Make humans more like God.
- Write a book or start a magazine (retranslating the Bible is optional).
- Put in a bunch of rules and regulations.
- Blend together with ideas from other religions.

Then all you do is let the whole thing bake (or half-bake) for a few years and *voilà!* You will have your own religion.

Nothing New Under the Sun

Even though the religions we're going to talk about in this chapter are relatively new (that is, less than 200 years old), the whole idea of setting up your own belief system as a way of getting around God is as old as humanity itself. In fact, it started when the first two humans, Adam and Eve, told God that they wanted to be just like Him (Genesis 3:5-6). Later, God's own people, the Jews, got tired of doing what God wanted them to do, so they decided to do "whatever seemed right in their own eyes" (Judges 21:25). In the first century, when religions were built around everything from turtles to Roman emperors, the apostle Paul observed that many people preferred to worship "the things God made but not the Creator himself" (Romans 1:25). It's an old, old story.

As wise King Solomon wrote, "History merely repeats itself. It has all been done before. Nothing under the sun is truly new" (Ecclesiastes 1:9). Which brings us to the blended-belief cults in this chapter: Christian Science, the Unity School of Christianity, and the United Church of Religious Science. The founders of these religions, known collectively as the "mind sciences," used the ingredients we listed, but with a twist. They believed that the human mind is the most powerful thing in the universe, even more powerful than God.

I Think, Therefore I Am Great

Before we look at the mind sciences and what they believe, we need to understand something very important. The idea that the human mind is above everything else did not originate with the mind-science cults, and the influence of this kind of thinking goes way beyond the particular beliefs of the one million or so people who are officially affiliated with the three main mind-science churches. You'll find it in philosophy, science, politics, and the popular culture.

It all started with the French, or at least a French philosopher and mathematician by the name of René Descartes (1596–1650), who decided that in order to figure out the world, all you need is reason and math. The way you prove that things exist is to think about them. Descartes used this philosophy to prove his own existence ("I think, therefore I am"), as well as to prove the existence of God ("I think about God, therefore He exists"). Before Descartes came on the scene, people thought you needed faith to believe in God. Descartes argued that all you need is reason.

The Day the Apple Fell

Not long after Descartes was doing his thinking in France, Sir Isaac Newton (1642–1727) was making huge contributions in the field of science over in England. We all know Newton for coming up with the law of universal gravitation after an apple clunked him on the head, but he was much more than a guy who hung out in orchards. Newton's total body of work (he also invented calculus, much to the chagrin of students everywhere) did more to advance science than anything before or since.

To the people of his day, Newton wasn't just conducting science experiments or writing math theories. He was unlocking the secrets of the natural world. His astounding discoveries sparked the Age of Enlightenment (sometimes referred to as the Age of Reason) in both Europe and the American colonies. As the eighteenth century unfolded, the leading thinkers of the world were convinced that thinking and reason and the mind were the keys to the universe. Humankind was finally coming out of the Dark Ages into a new era of enlightenment. Almost overnight, reason became more important than religion.

*T*he first person to write the story of the falling apple that gave Newton the idea of gravitation was Voltaire.

Who Needs God?

Not to be outdone by the British, the French stepped back into the limelight when the philosopher Voltaire (1694–1778) became a poster boy for the Age of Enlightenment. Voltaire believed in the power of human reason, science, and respect for all humanity, but he took these one step further. Through a number of brilliant books, he denounced supernaturalism (that is, "beyond the natural world"), religion, and the clergy. In short, Voltaire hated Christianity, although he believed in the existence of God.

We the People

The Age of Enlightenment effectively ended in Europe with the French Revolution in 1789, but it was just getting started in America. Thomas Jefferson (1743–1826) was greatly influenced by reason and the concepts of the Enlightenment, especially those regarding the rights and freedoms of the individual. As the author of the United States Constitution, Jefferson believed that democracy would succeed only if people made reasonable choices.

Jefferson and God

Those of us living in America sometimes state that our country was founded on Christian principles. More accurately, it was founded on the principle of *deism*. Many of America's founding fathers, including Jefferson and Benjamin Franklin, were deists. They believed that God created the universe but then left the universe to run on its own. God exists, but He is not personal. Because God is not involved in history or in the lives of individuals, it's up to us to make our own way through reason and effort. By contrast, the idea that God created the world and is personally involved with it is called *theism*.

New Thoughts for a New Age

One of the stepchildren of this marriage between European enlightenment and American deism was a movement called New Thought. It took philosophy, science, and religion to an entirely different level by emphasizing metaphysics and mental healing. The man who is considered the founder of the New Thought movement was Phineas Parkhurst Quimby (1802–1866). He believed that all sickness originated in the mind and was a consequence of false beliefs. Originally a student of hypnosis, Quimby believed he could heal physical diseases by mere suggestion. Of course, the person being healed had to be open to the wisdom of God, which he called "the Christ."

Now, this wasn't *the* Christ as in Jesus Christ, but rather an impersonal principle of the mind. To Quimby, the human Jesus was just a human being who used the Christ principle to heal people. Jesus isn't our Savior, but merely our example.

*B*efore — Dr. Hazen Adds…

*B*efore Quimby set up his mental healing practice in Portland, Maine, he had a popular traveling mesmerism act in which he would put his young companion, Lucius Burkmar, into a trance and then have Lucius prescribe strange cures to the sick folks in the audience.

After Quimby died, the New Thought movement continued to develop, and its teachings were formalized by the Divine Science Church, which taught:

- God is the sole reality.

- Sickness is the failure to realize this truth.

- Healing comes when you realize that the human race is one with God.

At its core, the New Thought belief system was nothing more than *pantheism,* which is the belief that all is God. There's no such thing as a personal Creator who exists independent of His creation, yet in dynamic relationship with it. God is more like a "universal life force" or an "infinite idea." The life of God and the life of man are the same, so in essence man is God. This is taken right from Hinduism (see chapter 7). In fact, two of America's most articulate spokesmen for pantheism were the influential writers Henry David Thoreau and Ralph Waldo Emerson, who was a student of Hinduism.

*W*hat *I*s *M*etaphysics?

Metaphysics is a branch of philosophy that deals with the nature of ultimate reality.

It's Not Your Mind and It's Not Science

The term *mind science* sounds so intellectual. In fact, it's anti-intellectual. As Ron Rhodes points out, the word *mind* refers to God as the Divine Mind, and *science* doesn't mean physical science, but rather metaphysical science of a mental nature. "Mind science groups advocate that Divine Mind fills all reality and that we should seek to harmonize our mind with it so we become one with it."

But we digress. Our point is to connect Quimby and the New Thought movement in all of its pantheistic glory to the mind sciences. Fortunately, that's already been done. Cult expert Ron Rhodes calls Quimby the "father of the mind sciences" because he and his metaphysical, mind healing, pantheistic beliefs had a direct influence on each of the three founders of the mind sciences.

Mind Science Takes Root

We're going to look at each of the mind sciences in order of their beginnings. As you learn about the founders, keep in mind (and by *mind* we mean the ability that God gave you to think for yourself) that all three of these cults share these basic beliefs:

- God is an impersonal principle, or Divine Mind.
- The Divine Mind is all that is real.
- The material world doesn't exist; it is only a part of the Divine Mind.

Christian Science

Although it is not the largest, Christian Science is probably the best-known of the mind sciences. And even though it has experienced a decline in membership and revenue over the last decade, Christian Science remains an influential religion. You can find Christian Science Reading Rooms on busy streets in most major cities, and for years the *Christian Science Monitor* has been a respected newspaper, although its circulation today is less than 75,000.

A Quick Look at the Mind Sciences

	Christian Science	Unity School of Christianity	United Church of Religious Science
Founder	Mary Baker Eddy	Charles and Myrtle Fillmore	Ernest S. Holmes
Date Founded	1879	1891	1927
Current Membership	250,000	110,000	600,000
Primary Literature	*Science and Health with Key to the Scriptures* (book); *Christian Science Monitor* (newspaper)	*Metaphysical Bible Dictionary* (book); *Daily Word* (devotional magazine)	*The Science of Mind* (book); *Science of Mind* (magazine)
View of God	God is an impersonal Divine Mind. All is God.	God is the impersonal Divine Mind and Principle. God is in all things.	God is an impersonal Force or Principle. God is in all things.

The Christian Science religion was founded by Mary Baker Eddy, who was born in 1821 in New Hampshire. Mary Baker was a sickly child who got involved in spiritualism and occultism as an adult. In 1862 she went to see the mind healer Phineas Quimby for a case of spinal inflammation. She claimed that she was healed of her affliction.

Eddy became a student of Quimby's unique brand of metaphysics and mental healing, eventually blending his concepts with her own ideas. In 1875, nine years after Quimby died, Eddy published a book (something Quimby never did). She claimed that the ideas in *Science and Health with Key to the Scriptures* came from a new revelation. In fact, an article in a 1904 edition of the *New York Times* showed that much of the book was plagiarized from Quimby.

Eddy established the Massachusetts Metaphysical College, where she taught her principles to 4000 students over a period of eight years, and in 1879 she founded the Church of Christ, Scientist in Boston. By the time she died in 1910, the church had a million members, far more than it does today. Still, there are currently 2300 Christian Science churches worldwide, with 1600 in the United States.

Negative Press

The Christian Science Church has traditionally advised its members to choose its mental healing techniques rather than consulting a physician. Some high-profile court cases in the early 1990s revealed that 18 children had died needlessly as a result of parents following this teaching. According to Walter Martin, there were several court cases in which church members were charged with "manslaughter, murder, and child abuse for choosing prayer over medical treatment for illness." As a result of losing some of those cases (not to mention the negative publicity), the leadership of the Christian Science Church softened "its strong prohibition against medical treatment."

Unity School of Christianity

Myrtle Fillmore was introduced to Quimby's New Thought metaphysics at a lecture given in 1886 by one of Quimby's followers. She had tuberculosis and was desperately seeking a cure. At the lecture Myrtle learned that a "child of God" does not get sick. She immediately embraced this belief and claimed she experienced a complete healing. Soon Myrtle was reading every piece of New Thought and Christian Science literature she could find.

Meanwhile her husband, Charles, was engaged in his own study of metaphysics, occultism, Hinduism, and Christian Science. In 1889 he started a magazine called *Thought,* which included articles on every religion he could find. A year later Charles claimed he had a vision in which he heard a voice that said, "Unity." Charles liked the name, because he had been thinking about starting a new religion that took ideas from all the other religions. In 1891 Charles and Myrtle did just that, and the Unity School of Christianity was born.

While Unity has only 300 churches and just over 100,000 members, it has an aggressive mailing program that sends out 33 million pieces of literature each year.

*O*ccultism is the belief in the power of such practices as astrology, alchemy, divination, and magic. The power is based on hidden knowledge about the universe and its hidden forces.

United Church of Religious Science

The fastest-growing of the mind-science cults is the United Church of Religious Science, sometimes referred to as Science of Mind. The church was founded by Ernest Holmes in 1927. Like Eddy and the Fillmores, Holmes was influenced by some of Quimby's students and had an interest in the occult. He wrote a 600-page book, *The Science of Mind,* and started a magazine called *Science Journal.*

A true twentieth-century man, Holmes spread his religion by speaking in person and on the radio. He gained the admiration of a number of politicians, celebrities, and clergy, including Dr. Norman Vincent Peale, author of *The Power of Positive Thinking.*

A Little of This and a Little of That

When you take the beliefs of the three mind sciences and lump them together (which is what we're going to do in this section), you find a number of striking similarities. This should not surprise us, given their common roots in New Thought. Besides the attachment to Quimby, you will also notice some elements of belief that are common in today's so-called New Age spirituality (more about that in chapter 10). The more you learn about these religions and beliefs, the more you begin to realize that people will go to great lengths to get around the truth of the Bible, which is the truth about God, Jesus, humanity, sin and salvation, and the afterlife. Let's do a little comparison between the Bible and what it teaches and the beliefs and teachings of the mind sciences.

I didn't like any of the religions I was acquainted with, and so I made up one that I did like.

Ernest Holmes

The Bible

There's no more trustworthy, reliable, and practical scripture than the Bible, the only divinely inspired written message from God to humankind (2 Timothy 3:16). The mind sciences take a much different view:

- *Christian Science* teaches that the Bible is no more important than a regular history book. If you interpret the Bible literally, it will lead you to "unbelief and hopelessness." The only way to interpret the Bible is *spiritually,* and to do that you need Eddy's "divinely inspired" book, *Science and Health with Key to the Scriptures.* According to Eddy, her book—not the Bible—contains "absolute Truth."

- In keeping with the Fillmores' smorgasbord religion, the *Unity School* believes that the Bible is fine, but to capture all the truth, you need to study the holy books of all the religions. And if you don't want to go to all that trouble, you can simply access the truth locked in your own being (either that, or get a copy of the Unity book, the *Metaphysical Bible Dictionary*).

- *Religious Science* teaches that there are many holy books, and they are all equal to the Bible as far as divine revelation goes (Holmes was very fond of the Hindu scriptures). Holmes taught that, ultimately, the Science of Mind is "the culmination of all religions."

God

The Bible reveals that God is the eternal (Isaiah 40:28), holy (Isaiah 6:3), all-powerful (Revelation 19:6), all-knowing (Proverbs 5:21), loving (1 John 4:7-9) Creator (Genesis 1:1) of the universe. By contrast, the mind sciences believe that God is an impersonal principle.

- *Christian Science* teaches that because God is all and all is God, and because God is Spirit, only the spirit is real. The material world does not exist—it is an illusion. The Trinity does not exist, just the Divine Principle, which is expressed in a trinity of its own: Life, Truth, and Love.

- The *Unity School* believes that everything visible is a manifestation of God, the one Spirit. God is not a being with life, love, intelligence, and power. God is the Divine Principle that lives in everything.

- *Religious Science* believes that the universe is the body of God, a view called *panentheism*. Every person is part of the universe, so every person is part of God. Holmes wrote, "Taking the best from all sources, Religious Science has access to the highest enlightenment of the ages."

Jesus

Every religion other than Christianity and every cult ever conceived has stripped Jesus of His divine nature. The Bible teaches that Jesus was fully God and fully man (Colossians 2:9). Here's what the mind sciences believe about Jesus:

- *Christian Science* follows Quimby's principle of "the Christ." Jesus was a human who merely possessed the "divine idea" of the Christ. Eddy taught that Jesus didn't save anybody when He died on the cross. Instead, we have to save ourselves through the metaphysical principles.

- The *Unity School* teaches that the human Jesus was different from the impersonal Christ principle. We are the same as Jesus, except that we haven't yet expressed the Christ principle as fully as Jesus did.

- *Religious Science* believes that Jesus merely showed us the way. Jesus embodied the Christ "consciousness," and we can do the same thing. Since there's no such thing as death (more about that later), Jesus never died on the cross. And if He didn't die, then there was no resurrection.

Humankind and Sin

In the Christian belief system, God created people in His image (Genesis 1:26-27), but our relationship with God was broken because of sin (Romans 3:23). The mind sciences see humankind differently:

- In the *Christian Science* belief system, we are part of God because God is in everything. We also possess the Divine Mind, which is good, so we don't sin. In fact, when you become one with the Divine Mind (the goal of Christian Science), not only do you not sin, but you don't get sick and die.

- The *Unity School* believes that all is in God, so there can't be any sin. The only sin is to believe in sin.

- *Religious Science* teaches that all human beings are divine. We don't sin; we simply make mistakes. The only sin is to be ignorant of our own divine nature.

Salvation

The Bible teaches that as sinners, all people need salvation. Without it, we will face judgment. Salvation is the only way to be made right with a holy God, and the only way to be saved is through the Person and work of Jesus Christ (Romans 5:8-10). Here is how the mind sciences view salvation:

- Life, Truth, and Love (the trinity of *Christian Science*) are the key to salvation. When you stop believing in the illusion of sickness and sin, you will be saved. Eddy flatly denied the notion of "faith without works." Instead, she wrote, "Man as God's idea is already saved."

- In the *Unity School,* sins are forgiven when you cease to sin by understanding that you are good.

- In *Religious Science*, God does not punish sin, so there's no need for salvation. "As we correct our mistakes, we forgive our own sins." Salvation is essentially a matter of the mind.

Death and the Afterlife

This is what the Bible teaches: Those who have believed in Jesus by faith will not die spiritually but live forever with God in heaven (John 3:16; 14:1-3). Those who reject Jesus will spend eternity in hell (Revelation 20:15). Here's how the mind sciences view death, heaven, and hell:

- *Christian Science* has an interesting take on this. First, there is no hell (although you can make your own hell through incorrect thinking), and heaven results from correct thinking. Death is merely a transition for the mind, which keeps on living so it can continue to correct the wrong thinking about sickness and death.

- The *Unity School* fully embraces the Hindu belief in reincarnation, although it is a little different. In Hinduism your works in this life (called *karma*) impact the quality of your life in the next life. Charles Fillmore taught that through a series of reincarnations you can become more like Jesus, who embodied the Christ principle. Eventually you don't need reincarnation any longer and you are saved. There is no hell. In the end, everyone is saved.

- According to *Religious Science*, heaven and hell are merely illusions we create in our own minds. Everyone is already saved, so all we have to do is rid our minds of the illusion and embrace the reality. If anything, heaven is already in us. We just need to realize it.

So What's the Appeal?

As we studied and evaluated the mind sciences, one of the questions we asked was: What's the appeal? (This is a good question to ask of any religion, because it shows respect for the religion and the people who follow it.) There are some very intelligent and sincere people who belong to these mind-science churches. What do they like about their beliefs?

S Dr. Hazen Adds...

o what's the appeal? Bruce and Stan ask a very good question here—one that I believe is not asked often enough about various religious beliefs. After some historical reflection on the circumstances surrounding the origin of New Thought, you may see that it doesn't seem quite so outlandish that someone would embrace these ideas and practices. For instance, going to Dr. Quimby to be treated for a persistent illness was at least worth a try. The alternative to Quimby was mainstream medicine, which in Quimby's day was still very primitive by today's standards. More often than not, traditional doctors just didn't have effective treatments to offer, and when they did, their treatments were usually far worse than the disease itself. Quimby's patients reported many cures—especially of "nervous" diseases—and hence this "scientific" demonstration was thought by many to put a stamp of approval on his religious theories as well.

We think the appeal of the mind sciences has to do with how they make people *feel*. The reality of our world is that there is sickness and suffering, but the mind-science religions say this is an illusion and merely the result of wrong thinking. We have to eliminate the "old thinking" that dwells on the negative and convert to the "new thinking" that leads to the mastery of disease and death. The mind sciences are full of compassionate, spiritually sensitive people who want to *feel* better about humanity and our world, so they deny the reality of a personal God and substitute the notion of an impersonal life force. It's not what you think that counts, but how you feel.

It's easy to see how appealing this belief is in our culture, and you don't even have to be a member of a mind-science church to buy into it. As an example, just look at the tremendous popularity and appeal of the Star Wars culture. We're not saying that George Lucas is an advocate of the mind sciences, but where did the idea of the "Force" come from? This is not a personal God, but rather an impersonal, universal life force that you access by feeling it. Luke Skywalker wasn't successful until he could "feel" the force. Only then could he hit the target and save the world.

In the same way, our observation is that the mind sciences make people feel better about life by creating an alternate reality. The only question you have to ask is whether or not this alternate reality is rooted in truth or fantasy.

What's That Again?

1. Starting your own religion is nothing new. We humans have been trying to get around God since the Garden.

2. The idea that the human mind and reason are above everything else blossomed in the Age of Enlightenment, which started with the French philosopher René Descartes.

3. One of the results of the Age of Enlightenment in America was the New Thought movement, started by Phineas Parkhurst Quimby, a mind healer who believed all sickness was a consequence of false belief.

4. All three of the mind sciences can trace their roots to Quimby's New Thought beliefs.

5. All three mind-science cults teach that God is an impersonal Divine Mind, and that the material world does not exist, but is only a part of the Divine Mind, which is all that exists.

6. Christian Science came directly out of New Thought. Mary Baker Eddy knew Quimby and adapted his ideas into her religion.

7. The Unity School of Christianity is a collection of ideas from many other religions.

8. According to founder Ernest Holmes, Religious Science is the "culmination of all other religions."

9. The appeal of the mind-science cults has to do with the way they make people feel.

Dig Deeper

The best book we found on the mind-science blended-belief cults is *The Challenge of the Cults* by Ron Rhodes. He is very thorough and objective in his analysis.

The Kingdom of the Cults by Walter Martin and other cult experts is also very thorough and heavily footnoted.

Alan W. Gomes is a professor at the Talbot School of Theology. His book *Truth and Error* includes a chapter on the mind sciences that uses a lot of Scripture to compare the claims of the mind-science cults to Christianity.

Dr. Hazen also recommends *Spirits in Rebellion* by Charles S. Braden and *Mind Sciences* by Todd Ehrenborg.

■ ■ ■

*Q*uestions for *R*eflection and *D*iscussion

1. If you were going to start and promote your own religion, what would be some of your basic beliefs, and what would be your marketing strategy?

2. What role should your intellect play in your faith?

3. Explain what happened to the concept of God during the Age of Enlightenment.

4. What is pantheism? How does it differ from theism?

5. Is the concept that "the material world does not exist" consistent with your experience? If that concept is true, then should we be bothered with constraints of morality and laws?

6. What do you think is the appeal of the mind sciences?

7. What arguments can you think of (pro and con) on the issue of whether all humanity is part of God because God is in everything?

■ ■ ■

Moving On . . .

Three thousand years ago King Solomon observed that there was nothing new under the sun. You are going to see a striking example of this in the next section on the philosophical religions, beginning with Hinduism, the oldest of them all. You're going to recognize that many of the ideas in Mormonism, Jehovah's Witnesses, and the mind sciences have their roots in the ancient religion from India.

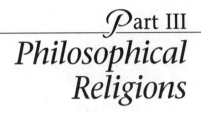

Part III
Philosophical Religions

Chapter 7

And instead of worshiping the glorious,
ever-living God, they worshiped
idols made to look like mere people,
or birds and animals and snakes.

Paul the apostle

Most people would be hard-pressed to describe the basic beliefs of the Hindu religion, but they could easily identify the influence of Hinduism in our popular culture, mainly because...

- Everybody knows what it means to have good *karma,* something that is very much a part of Hindu culture.

- All kinds of people (including many movie stars and rock musicians) practice *yoga,* a mainstay of Hinduism.

- The Hindu practice of *meditation* is a recurring theme on television and in the movies.

So is all of this dabbling in Hindu philosophy and practice pretty harmless, or is there more to it? Are the tolerant and inclusive ideas of Hinduism a healthy alternative to our materialistic and me-centered culture, or are they a doorway to something else? Let's find out in this chapter about one of the world's oldest and most influential religions.

Hinduism:
All Is One

*H*induism is the third most popular religion on earth. Thirteen percent of the world's population is Hindu, and 83 percent of the population of India is Hindu. Yet there is no central headquarters (such as Salt Lake City) or no single holy city (such as Jerusalem or Mecca). Technically, Hinduism isn't even a single religion, but rather a collection of interwoven beliefs that can trace their roots to the Hindu culture in India.

There isn't a stated creed or set of beliefs in Hinduism, and that's part of the appeal. Because it's free from absolute or formal doctrine, Hinduism is more or less a "designer" religion. You want to worship a god or several gods? No problem. Hinduism has plenty to go around. You would rather not mess with a god? That's cool. In Hinduism, gods are not essential.

What matters is attaining freedom from matter, or the world as we see it. The idea is to eliminate any ties to the material plane of existence and to understand how you are personally related to the spiritual whole. Historically, the two mantras of Hinduism have been "All is One" and "All is God."

Hindu Terms You Already Know

Those of us in the Western Hemisphere know more about Hinduism than we think. In the preceding paragraph we used the word *mantra* to indicate repetition. In fact, *mantra* is a term used by practitioners of Transcendental Meditation (a derivative of Hinduism) to chant or repeat certain words in order to invoke the presence of a particular god. Similarly, people sometimes use the word *karma* to indicate good or bad fortune. Actually, *karma* is more closely related to *reincarnation,* a huge Hindu concept. We even have been exposed to *Vishnu,* one of the Big Three Hindu gods. In "The Simpsons," the long-running cartoon sitcom, Apu Nahasapeemapetilon is the Hindu proprietor of Kwik-E-Mart. Apu keeps a statue of Vishnu in the back room.

But we're getting ahead of ourselves. Before we can sort out the various terms, beliefs, gods, and philosophies of Hinduism, we need a brief history lesson.

Origins of Hinduism

Hinduism has no specific founder or historical event to mark its beginning, so it's nearly impossible to come up with a date for when Hinduism began. Scholars know that about 4000 years ago a highly developed civilization known as the Mohenjo-Daro was flourishing in the Indus River Valley in northwest India. The people of this civilization were known as Dravidians. From archaeological digs we know they were fairly advanced and probably pacifists (there's no evidence of weaponry).

This apparently made the Dravidians easy pickings for the invading Aryans, who, it is thought, came down from Persia (present-day Iran) in 1500 B.C. and basically assimilated the

A Quick Look at Hinduism

- The word *Hindu* comes from the Sanskrit word *shindu,* meaning "river," and more specifically, the Indus River.

- There are 790,000,000 Hindus worldwide.

- Thirteen percent of the world's population is Hindu.

- More than 80 percent of the people of India practice some form of Hinduism.

- Nepal, where 89 percent of the population is Hindu, is the only nation where Hinduism is the state religion.

- One million Hindus live in the United States, primarily in major cities such as New York, Los Angeles, and the San Francisco Bay Area.

Dravidian culture into their own. The Aryan religious practices were mixed with those of the Dravidians, producing these fundamental principles:

- belief in reincarnation

- the worship of a diverse group of gods who took various forms

- belief in the essential spiritual unity of humankind

You can see elements of *polytheism* (literally, "many gods") and *monism* (there is only one ultimate reality, and we are all part of it) in these early beliefs that formed the foundation for Hinduism.

Early Hindu Scriptures

The Aryan religion was expressed in hymns, prayers, and chants and collected in sacred texts known as the Vedas. Vedic literature was composed from 1400 to 400 B.C., and it passed down through the centuries until was finally written down in the fourteenth century A.D. The spoken language of the Aryans was Sanskrit, so that was the language of the Vedas (it was also considered to be the language of the gods). *Veda* is a Sanskrit word that means "knowledge." Hindus consider the Vedas to be supernaturally inspired.

Early Vedic religion was devoted to ritual and sacrifice to many gods, but later Vedas moved more toward *pantheism* (*pan*, meaning "everything," and *theos*, meaning "God"). The basic idea of pantheism is that God is the world, and the world is God.

*W*hat in the *W*orld?

Here's what else was going on in the world when the Aryans invaded the Dravidians in 1500 B.C.:

- The Egyptian civilization was thriving.
- Moses was born in 1526 B.C.
- In 1446 B.C. Moses led the Jews out of captivity in Egypt.
- God gave the Ten Commandments to the people of Israel in 1445 B.C.

The Big Three

As Hinduism developed, most of the early Hindu deities disappeared (where they went, nobody knows) and were replaced by three primary gods:

- *Brahma*—This is the main god, known as the "Impersonal Absolute" and the "Ultimate Reality" (these would be good names for a WWF wrestler). By 1000 B.C., Brahma had become so important that an entire order of priests known as the Brahmins developed.

- *Vishnu*—Here is Apu's god, the champion of all good causes. Vishnu rules in heaven and rules over earth as the preserver. According to religious expert George Braswell, Vishnu has been compared to the Christian concept of God. Vishnu has taken many human forms (also known as *avatars*), the most popular of which is Krishna.

- *Shiva*—The third god of the Hindu Big Three takes on many roles, including creator and destroyer. Shiva signifies the eternal life-death rhythm of the universe. A popular Hindu idol or image of Shiva shows him with four arms.

𝒯he 𝓜any 𝓕orms of 𝓥ishnu

Krishna is the human incarnation of Vishnu and one of the most popular of all Hindu deities. Stories of Krishna are told in the Bhagavad Gita, India's most popular sacred book. The "Gita" has been called the "New Testament of India" and even the "Gospel of Krishna." Vishnu has also taken on these animal forms: fish, turtle, boar, man-lion, horse, and dwarf.

Brahmins Rule

When you are the main religious guys devoted to the biggest god, you tend to become the Big Cheese (not an official Hindu title). This is what happened to the Brahmin priests. For 500 years the Brahmins supervised the practices of temple worship and ritual. They became the keepers of the ultimate reality and in so doing became very powerful, even to the point of climbing to the highest social class.

Eventually the priests ensured their position at the top of the Hindu food chain by creating a complicated system of social classes, also known as *castes*. The rules of the caste system were known as *Varna*. Since the priests claimed that it was divine revelation, Varna became part of Hindu religious law, effectively dividing all of Indian society. The *Brahmins* (priests) were the highest class, followed by the *Kshatriyas* (warriors and rulers), the *Vaisyas* (merchants and artists), and the *Shudras* (slaves). Within each of these four castes were hundreds of subcastes, each with a certain rank. Only the top three castes were allowed to practice Hinduism. The Shudras weren't even allowed to hear the Vedas.

Rebellion and Revival

By 500 B.C. the caste system had become so oppressive that some influential Hindu leaders began to break away from the religious tyranny of the Brahmin priests. Siddhartha Gautama (the Buddha, also known as "the enlightened one") denounced the Varna caste system and started a new religion in India that later flourished in China (see chapter 8).

Don't Touch Them

One of the cruelest by-products of the caste system was the group of people known as the Untouchables. Actually, they weren't even treated as people. The Untouchables were so far below the Shudras that they were completely outside the social order. Untouchables always had the dirtiest jobs and were reduced to literally eating and drinking the dregs of the earth. The Indian government outlawed discrimination against the Untouchables in 1947—the same year India became a nation—but Untouchables are still a part of Indian society to this day. Ironically, the Untouchables were descended from the Dravidians, the original inhabitants of India. In the 1930s the Indian nationalist leader Mohandas Gandhi began referring to Untouchables as *Harijans,* which means "children of God."

Meanwhile another set of Hindu scriptures, known as the Upanishad, gained popularity and prompted a kind of revival among the followers of Brahma. The appeal of the Upanishad (the last of the Vedas) was its emphasis on inner meditation rather than outward performance. Instead of a priest commanding the people to perform rituals, spiritual teachers known as *gurus* started instructing spiritual seekers. The word *Upanishad* literally means "to sit near to."

The Upanishad also spawned a major school of thought known as *Vedanta.* This philosophy of the Upanishad reinforced the idea that there is unity in diversity. Behind all the many gods is the one reality of Brahman. This is the essence of monism, which Walter Martin describes this way:

Every aspect of the universe, both animate and inanimate, shares the same essentially divine nature. There is actually only one Self in the universe.

Because the philosophy of Vedanta became such a major influence in Hinduism, we're going to look at it in more detail. Don't skip over this part. This is where Hinduism really gets interesting.

The Wheel of Misfortune

Even though the philosophies of Hinduism can vary widely, there are two beliefs you can count on when talking to a practitioner of the Hindu religion: reincarnation and karma.

- *Reincarnation*—Hindus believe there are two types of souls. There is the individual soul, known as *atman,* which is eternal and uncreated. And there is the Universal Soul, known as *Brahman.* One of the major goals of Hinduism is for the individual soul to unite with the Universal Soul, and therefore become one with the ultimate reality. In order for this to happen, the atman must die and be born again time after time into the world in different bodies (some Hindus believe you can come back as an animal or a plant). This death-birth cycle is called reincarnation, or the "transmigration of the soul." In Hindu terms it's called *samsara.*

  The ultimate goal of Hinduism is to break free from this wheel of misfortune by uniting with the Universal Soul. This is called *moksha.* How does this happen? That's where *karma* comes in.

- *Karma*—The law of karma has to do with good works and bad works (or if you prefer, good karma and bad karma). The more good karma you can produce, the better your chances of attaining freedom from the reincarnation nightmare. However, if the individual soul produces more bad karma than good karma, then you are destined to die and come back as a horsefly. The bad news about bad karma is that it carries over into the next life. But then, good karma also carries over, so there's motivation to produce good works.

I'll Have a Moksha, Please

As we said, the ultimate goal of the Hindu is to attain *moksha*, which is freedom from *samsara* when you finally unite with *Brahman* (hey, we're getting pretty good at using these Hindu terms). This happens when you've got way more good karma than bad karma. So far, so good. And how do you pick up the good karma? Well, there are three classic ways (called *margas*) in Hinduism to attain good works: the way of activity *(karma marga)*, the way of knowledge *(jnana marga)*, and the way of devotion *(bhatki marga)*. Braswell writes, "One may choose one or several of these ways in hope of breaking the birth cycle and experiencing ultimate freedom."

Karma and the Caste System

One of the unfortunate effects of the Hindu belief in reincarnation and karma is that it has perpetuated the caste system in India. The only way to move up to a higher caste is to be reincarnated into that caste. And the only way to do that is to be obedient to the rules of the caste you are in. For example, if a Shudra wanted to move up to the level of a Vaisyas, he would have to be a very good Shudra and hope for a promotion in his next life. Winfried Corduan writes, "To shortcut the system and attain a higher standard of living would violate the structures of the caste and thereby only incur worse karma." The reality of karma is that it prevents people from attempting to rise to a higher caste or help members of other castes.

The Way of Activity

This way to ultimate freedom is a popular form of Hinduism, and it is best summarized by "daily duty." You build up good karma by fulfilling certain religious and social obligations. On the religious side, a good Hindu will worship gods, goddesses, and spirits through ceremonies that take place both in the temple and at home. The Brahmin priests oversee the worship and ceremonies in the temples, which are often paid for by wealthy Hindus who want to build up good karma.

Each temple has a god who takes the form of an idol or image. It's the Brahmin's job to wake up the god, talk to it by chanting, bathe it, and offer it flowers, food, and incense. Families can also worship a god at home. Typically the idol is kept in a box, and the family members pretty much do the same things as the temple priests: They worship the god by waking, bathing, feeding, and chanting to it. All of this helps build up good karma.

On the social side, a good Hindu must be very careful to stay within the caste. This means working and marrying within the caste, eating or not eating certain foods, and raising children who will do the same.

*M*oksha is sometimes translated as "redemption."

The Way of Knowledge

This way is the least popular form of Hinduism because it is quite a bit more mystical and much more difficult than the way of activity. First taught in the Upanishads, the way of knowledge is based on the belief that you can experience the unity of the individual soul with the Universal Soul through the practice of yoga meditation.

When we Westerners hear the word *yoga*, we think of it as a form of stretching and relaxation with a few "Oms" thrown in for good measure. This is a far cry from the Hindu practice of yoga meditation. As Braswell explains, there are four stages through which one must pass to accomplish the way of knowledge, and all of them involve a *guru*.

- *Stage one* is the *student stage*. Here the young Hindu studies the Veda scriptures, especially the Upanishads.

- *Stage two* is the *householder stage*. This is when the man gets married and raises his family.

- *Stage three* is the *forest dweller stage*. If a Hindu man wants to continue the way of knowledge (it's his choice), then he gives his property to his family, asks his sons to care for his wife, and leaves home for the forests. He finds a guru and devotes himself to meditation, far from the distractions of the world.

- *Stage four* is the *ascetic stage,* where the Hindu has learned all he can from the guru and is now ready to practice yoga on his own. Braswell writes:

> Yoga provides the Hindu with the method to reach freedom. The Yoga posture with head erect and spine straight and breath control enables the Hindu to attain supreme concentration. Through gazing upon certain sacred symbols and reciting certain sacred sounds, the Hindu approaches mystical union with the absolute, the world soul.

Another way to achieve supreme concentration is through self-torture. You know those pictures you see of a Hindu lying on a bed of thorns or staring into the sun until he goes blind? These are people in this stage trying to concentrate on the ultimate reality by renouncing their bodies.

*G*urus, *M*aharishis, and *S*wamis

In the Hindu tradition, gurus possess the secrets of the universe, the gods, and life itself. In order to learn how to properly meditate and practice yoga, you need to learn from a guru master. The titles of swami and maharishi are more specific designations for gurus. Maharishis often leave India and go to other countries in order to establish schools of meditation. In most major cities in America you can find a Hindu guru who is ready to teach his disciples the techniques of yoga, as well as the beliefs and practices of Hinduism.

The Way of Devotion

Before looking at the third path to moksha, let's review the first two ways. As we have seen in other belief systems, a works-based salvation is appealing to people who want to earn their way to

Where Do Hare Krishna and Transcendental Meditation Fit In?

If there's one Hindu deity that has crossed from East to West, it's Krishna. Not only is he popular in India, but Krishna has also become very visible in Europe and the United States, thanks to the efforts of the Hare Krishna. In 1965 Swami Bhaktivedanta Prabhupada came to New York City to establish the International Society for Krishna Consciousness (the official name for Hare Krishna). His timing could not have been better. If you know anything about the 1960s (someone once said that if you remember the sixties, you weren't really there), you know about the drug and youth counterculture. Society was in turmoil as young people rebelled against what they saw as materialistic, hypocritical Western values. The Swami offered a simpler, sweeter, more mystical spiritual experience. Braswell writes, "Hare Krishna became a missionary movement within the religious pluralism stream of America."

George Harrison of the Beatles became a fan. He even wrote a song about Krishna called "My Sweet Lord." In 1968 Harrison led his band mates on a pilgrimage to the Himalayan foothills of India, where they meditated at the feet of Maharishi Mahesh Yogi. Soon all kinds of celebrities were jumping on the Maharishi Express, and millions of Westerners bought into his brand of Hinduism, known as Transcendental Meditation. The Maharishi and his TM trainers weren't stupid. They marketed TM as something you could practice within your own religious belief system. The truth is that TM leads its practitioners to become one with the "Creative Intelligence." Similarly, true Hare Krishna devotees (the ones in orange robes you used to see in airports passing out the Swami's magazine *Back to Godhead*) withdraw from the world in order to devote themselves entirely to Krishna.

heaven. The problem with this path is that the Hindu never knows for sure if his good works are good enough (sounds like Islam, doesn't it?). The second path, the way of knowledge, looks good on paper, and there's something very cool about becoming a yoga master (like you, we've watched too many Star Wars movies). But let's face it, that's a tough way to go. Only a very few people have the guts to leave their homes and families only to eventually end up on a bed of thorns (you know what they say: "No guts, no glory").

That leaves us with the way of devotion, also known as *bhatki*. This is the most popular belief and practice in Hinduism because you get to choose your own god, and there are millions to choose from (as many as 330 million, but who's counting?). The most common choice is Vishnu, the god of incarnations, and the most popular incarnated god (or avatar) is Krishna. To the Hindu, Krishna offers freedom from the karma wheel of misfortune through love and grace toward the individual, as long as the individual gives love and devotion to Krishna.

Followers of Krishna see the relationship between themselves and the deity in a different way. A Hindu can keep his identity and become dependent upon the deity rather than trying to become one with the deity.

It's easy to understand why this way of devotion ranks number one with Hindus. You don't have to go through all those rituals every day, you can stay home with the wife and kids, and there's no need to torture yourself or stay in the yoga position for half the day. "Devotion and grace work hand in hand to provide good Karma, break the transmigration of the soul, and enable the Hindu to attain liberation," Braswell writes.

Hinduism and Christianity

Did you ever think that learning about an old and complicated religion like Hinduism could give you insights into some of the thinking going on in our culture today? It's true! Not only does an understanding of Hinduism give you a handle on other Eastern religions, including Buddhism and its derivatives, but it also helps you better understand the New Age belief systems that are all around you today. We're going to talk about the New Age beliefs in chapter 10, but you need to know now that many of the Hindu concepts we discussed in this chapter are a part of many other belief systems.

Let's review some of these concepts and then respond to them from the viewpoint of biblical Christianity.

- ***There are many gods, not just one God.*** Polytheism is a central belief in Hinduism. Different gods perform different functions, and not one is personal. This belief opens the door to relativism, meaning that the truth is what you decide it is. Just like Hindus can choose the god or gods they want, they can choose what they want to believe.

  At the core of Christian belief is the concept of one true God, who is eternal, all-powerful, all-knowing, all-loving, holy, and personal. Because God is the Creator of the heavens and the earth, He is responsible for the unseen as well as the material world. Furthermore, God exists independently of His creation, and the universe is completely dependent on Him. God fills the universe with His presence and power, but He is not the universe. God is not in everything, and everything is not God. A rock is not God, and neither are you.

- ***There is only one ultimate reality.*** It's interesting that from its polytheistic roots, Hinduism developed the concept of Brahma, the impersonal creator of the world, and Brahman, the Universal Soul and ultimate reality. Ron Rhodes points out that this concept of pantheistic monism (all is God and God is one) contradicts polytheism: "Both of these positions cannot be true at the same time. If all is God, then there cannot be many different gods."

  The Bible teaches that before the beginning of the universe, God existed in "tri-unity"—Father, Son, and Holy Spirit. God created the universe, culminating with the creation of people in His image (Genesis 1:26-27). The Bible is the historical record of God's interaction with humankind. The reality is that a real, personal God wants a relationship with His image-bearing created beings.

And there's the whole matter of humankind's eternal destiny. In the Hindu system you are basically absorbed into Brahman, the Universal Soul. In the Christian belief system, we have the opportunity to have an eternal and personal relationship with the Creator of the universe. It doesn't get any better than that.

- *Reincarnation is the way to become one with the ultimate reality.* If reincarnation were real, then why hasn't the human race improved? After thousands upon thousands of reincarnation cycles, you would think that eventually all the bad karma would disappear, but that hasn't happened. The fact is that the human moral condition has gotten worse, not better. There are more wars, not fewer. There is more suffering, not less. In India in particular, where 83 percent of the people are Hindu, there is more suffering than in any nation on earth.

    The Bible clearly teaches that each human being lives and dies once, and then faces judgment (Hebrews 9:27). There are no second lives or chances. When Jesus talked about being "born again" (John 3:3), He was referring to a spiritual rebirth, not the physical rebirth cycle.

- *Good works will ultimately save you.* The whole system of Vedanta is based on karma, or works. If your good works outweigh your bad works, then you have a better shot at salvation. In Hinduism, there's no such thing as sinning against a holy God. Life is lived in the scales of good and bad, and in the cycle of reincarnation. Acts of wrongdoing do not offend any god, but are simply the result of ignorance.

    The Christian concept of salvation is that works cannot save us. Only by faith alone in the Person and work of Jesus can we be saved to an eternal relationship with God. Good works are the evidence or the result of salvation, not the cause.

    In Hinduism, you never know where you stand. No one knows from one day to another (or from one life to another) if his or her works are good enough to break free from the karma cycle. In Christianity, everyone is on the same level: We're all guilty of offending a holy God, and the only way any of us can be saved is by His grace (Ephesians 2:8-10).

> Fritz Ridenour writes that the great Indian leader Mohandas Gandhi, "could not accept the Christian answer to the problem of sin, yet he felt a deep hunger for real salvation from sin." Ridenour quotes Gandhi:
>
>> For it is an unbroken torture to me that I am still so far from Him, who, as I fully know, governs every breath of my life, and whose offspring I am.

• *Vishnu is the god of grace and love.* We find it interesting to compare the qualities of Vishnu with the Person of Christ. We're not saying they are the same, but why is it that Hindus have assigned the Christlike qualities of love, grace, and a personal relationship to their god Vishnu? We think it's because Hindus—like all people—long for a God who can love them and relate to them on a personal level, perhaps even living among them.

That's exactly what Jesus came to earth to do. Jesus is the visible image of the invisible God (Colossians 1:15). Jesus is God with skin on, who came to live with us for a while so we could experience God personally. Hindus believe in the incarnation of many gods. The Bible teaches that God became incarnate only once through the Person of Jesus (John 1:14). Jesus is not one of many. He is unique and the only way back to God (John 14:6).

Glossary of Hindu Names and Terms

Atman	The eternal, individual soul
Avatar	An incarnation of a Hindu god. Krishna is an avatar of Vishnu. An avatar can take on the form of a human or animal.
Bhagavad Gita	The most popular Hindu scripture. It tells the story of Krishna and has been called the New Testament of Hinduism.
Bhatki	The "way of devotion" and the most popular path to moksha
Brahma	The creator god and the number one god in the Hindu pantheon
Brahman	The Universal Soul, the ultimate reality
Brahmins	The priests of Brahma and the highest Hindu caste
Caste	The system of social hierarchy among Hindus in India
Dharma	Hindu laws that explain the true ways of the gods—can also refer to religious obligations or individual virtue.
Guru	A Hindu spiritual teacher or guide
Karma	Works, either good or bad. Karma determines future lives.
Krishna	The human incarnation of Vishnu
Kshatriyas	The second highest caste—includes warriors and rulers
Mantra	A word or hymn, usually in the Sanskrit language, which practitioners of Hindu meditation say over and over again to conjure up the gods
Margas	The "ways" or paths to moksha
Moksha	The freedom one experiences when the atman unites with the Brahman
Om	The ultimate Hindu syllable and the favorite Hindu mantra

Samsara	The transmigration of the soul where one life cycles to another; reincarnation
Sanskrit	The language of the Aryans—considered to be the language of the gods by Hindus. The Vedas are written in Sanskrit.
Shiva	The third god of the Big Three Hindu gods—depicted with four arms
Shudras	The lowest Hindu caste—includes slaves
Untouchables	People in India who exist below the Hindu caste system—considered subhuman. Their ancestors were aboriginal Dravidians.
Upanishads	The last of the Vedic literature—emphasizes inner meditation over outward performance
Vaisyas	The third rung on the Hindu caste ladder—includes merchants and artists
Varna	Rules of the caste system developed by the Brahmins
Vedanta	The Hindu philosophy that reinforced reincarnation and karma as the way to unite with the ultimate reality
Vedas	Sacred Hindu scriptures given by the gods to Hindu holy men—usually expressed in hymns or rituals
Vishnu	The Hindu god that preserves—has many avatars
Yoga	Physical or mental means to achieve unity with the Universal Soul
Yugo	Inexpensive car originally manufactured in Yugoslavia—has nothing to do with Hinduism, but we wanted to see if you were paying attention

What's That Again?

1. Hinduism is a major world religion with no founder and no single creed or doctrine.

2. The main goal of the Hindu is to break free from the world as we see it to unite with the ultimate reality.

3. Ancient Hindus believed in reincarnation, polytheism, and the essential spiritual unity of humankind.

4. The most important Hindu scriptures are the Vedas, composed over a thousand-year period beginning in 1400 B.C.

5. The three main Hindu gods are Brahma, Vishnu, and Shiva. The priests of Brahma, called Brahmins, climbed to the top of the religious and social order and established the Hindu system of castes.

6. The philosophy of Vedanta, which became the driving force of Hinduism, came out of the Upanishads, the last of the Vedas. This school of thought teaches that the only way for the individual soul to unite with the Universal Soul is through reincarnation and karma.

7. Moksha occurs when the individual soul finally unites with the Universal Soul. There are three ways to attain moksha: the way of activity, the way of knowledge, and the way of devotion.

8. Understanding the beliefs of Hinduism can help you understand many of the other religions and belief systems of the world.

Dig Deeper

We really had to dig to make sense out of the richly textured religion of Hinduism. When it was all said and done (and written), we found these three books to be most helpful:

Hinduism by J. Isamu Yamamoto is an excellent resource. The beliefs of Hinduism (along with Hare Krishna and Transcendental Meditation) are carefully outlined, analyzed, and refuted.

George W. Braswell is a professor of world religions, so he knows his stuff. His book *Understanding World Religions* is concise and easy to follow.

Neighboring Faiths by Winfried Corduan is unique in that it does more than just discuss the beliefs of Hinduism (and other religions that are a part of our Western culture). He shows how each religion is practiced in daily life so you can easily put a human face to the impersonal beliefs.

■ ▨ ▣

*Q*uestions for *R*eflection and *D*iscussion

1. What is the primary appeal of Hinduism in North America? Give three examples of Hindu beliefs that have infiltrated popular culture. Is it possible to practice the beliefs of Hinduism without calling yourself a Hindu?

2. Explain the caste system. Has this been a positive or a negative outgrowth of Hinduism? Why?

3. In what contexts do you hear people use the word "karma"? What do you think people really mean when they use it? Is there a place for the concept of karma in Christianity? Why or why not?

4. Many people who want nothing to do with God practice yoga meditation. What's the appeal of yoga? What kind of common ground could you find with someone who practices yoga?

5. Explain how the Hindu concept of many gods conflicts with its belief in one ultimate reality.

6. Is reincarnation defensible from a rational standpoint? Why or why not?

7. Using the god of Vishnu, how would you explain Jesus Christ to a Hindu?

■ ■ ■

Moving On . . .

We hope you're enjoying this introduction to world religions. We've got to be honest and tell you that we were surprised at the relevance of Eastern religions like Hinduism. By "relevance" we don't mean that we relate to them. We just didn't know how influential these religions have become in our culture over the last few decades.

The reality is that the philosophies of Hinduism and Buddhism (the subject of our next chapter) aren't going to go away. As our world is shrinking, more and more people are being exposed to these ideas about God and reality and the world we live in. You can't just brush these religions aside. You will find elements of these belief systems in some of the popular books that you read, in many of the movies and television shows you watch, and in the thinking of some of the people you interact with at work and at school. So take a breath (or get some sleep), and then move on to the next chapter. There's much more to come.

Chapter 8

May I not enter into Nirvana until
I have brought all beings to
supreme enlightenment.

a Bodhisattva vow

Until about a decade or so ago, most people in the United States didn't have much contact with the Buddhist religion. Their only impression of it might have been those gaudy statues of a grinning, bald-headed Buddha with a huge beer belly near the entrance of most Chinese restaurants. Those statues were a bit scary, and most people didn't know how they should respond to them. Some thought they should nod as they passed by in a gesture of respect; others thought they should rub the belly for good luck. (As kids, we were the belly-rubbing types.)

Well, we have come a long way in the last ten years or so. Now, thanks to a few Hollywood celebrities, we realize that Buddhism is a religion that has appeal to people in the Western culture. And as a bestselling author and winner of the Nobel peace prize, the Dalai Lama has been on the covers of *Time* and *People* magazine (and we have to admit, he's rather photogenic with his stylish eyewear and bright orange robes). With all this exposure to Buddhism, we're no longer ignorant about it.

But wait a minute. While Buddhism has much more prominence in our culture, most people are too embarrassed to admit that they don't know anything at all about it. If you fall into this category, then this chapter is for you. We think you'll find the next few pages to be fascinating. After all, that statue of Buddha represents a lot more than just a silly grin and a big belly.

Buddhism:
From Ignorance to Enlightenment

*W*e are two guys who are always in search of wisdom. As our wives are quick to remind us, however, wishing for it doesn't make it so. (Of course, we learned *that* lesson in our youth when it was athleticism that we were interested in. Now we are content with more sedentary pursuits, like wisdom and a good vanilla latte.) We've always admired characters in the movies or on television that have been able to transcend conflict and turmoil in order to prevail through insightful wisdom or cleverness. Since we couldn't relate to Rambo or the tough-cop types, we gravitated to those martial arts gurus in the old Kung Fu television series or those Karate Kid movies. The lessons being taught to "Grasshopper" by the Buddhist monks or by Mr. Miyagi seemed to reveal a tranquility about life that brought everyone and everything into balance (and any remaining malcontents could be brought into line by a few swift martial arts moves to the side of their skulls).

That's part of the appeal of Buddhism. It represents a level of awareness that transcends the direct obstacles of life. Through the development of morality, meditation, and wisdom, you can reach a higher level that is the true nature of reality. This religious philosophy includes the concepts of reincarnation, karma, entering nirvana, and absolute liberation.

If you think this smacks a little of Hinduism, you're correct (and you are to be congratulated for remembering what you read in chapter 7). But even though Buddhism developed in India in the context of Hinduism, the two religions stand separate and apart from each other. The difference dates back to the beginning of Buddhism, when a young prince sneaked out of the palace for a look at real life.

An Escape Beyond the Palace Gate

It all started in the sixth century B.C. with the birth of Buddha, who was then known as Siddhartha Gautama. Actually, any self-respecting Buddhist recognizes that birth is just the continuation of a preexisting cycle, and Buddha spoke about his past existence, so technically the story really began long before the sixth century B.C., but let's not quibble about that.

The expectant parents were the rulers of a small kingdom in the region now known as Nepal. They had several indications that this was not going to be a typical kid, even for royalty. First of all, on the night of the conception of their child, the mother had a vision of a white elephant (the sign of an exceptional being) entering her womb. Then, before the birth, an astrologer gave the following prediction: The child would turn out to be a great world ruler, or, if he witnessed great suffering, he would become a great religious leader.

Siddhartha's father wanted his son to become a great world leader, so he did everything within his power to keep his son excluded from the suffering of the world. This meant that Siddhartha grew up behind the palace walls and never ventured out into the real world. He married a princess from another region, but their courtship and marriage were within the palace walls. This was a luxurious life that would have given most everyone else complete contentment. But not Siddhartha.

At the age of 29, with a wife and kids of his own, Siddhartha had to see what the rest of the world was like. He persuaded his chariot driver to take him on a drive through the village beyond the palace. On that brief trip, he saw—for the first time—an aged man, a sick man, a corpse being carried to cremation, and a wandering holy man. These "Four Signs" caused him to start thinking about old age, sickness, death, and the meaning of life. With knowledge of these realities, he could no longer live in the extravagance of the palace.

A Quick Look at Buddhism

- There are more than 350,000,000 Buddhists worldwide, although obtaining exact statistics is difficult because there are not organized churches in many regions and the religion is often attributed to all residents in an area.

- Buddhism is most prevalent in the countries of China, Japan, and Korea, and in Southeast Asia.

- With the growth of Asian ethnicities in the United States, the Buddhist population is increasing in the United States, with perhaps 500,000 followers. Buddhism is the main religion in Hawaii.

The Great Renunciation

After struggling within himself to reconcile the harsh realities of life with his own wealth and privilege, Siddhartha split from his family, shaved his head, and led a homeless life in the forest (an event now called the Great Renunciation). While in the forest, he met two holy men who taught him meditation. Hoping to find a spiritual dimension, Siddhartha decided to begin a long and strict fast until he reached the point where he could "feel his backbone through his stomach."

Despite all of his physical self-deprivation, he didn't obtain the spiritual enlightenment that he was seeking. He kept at this austere and ascetic lifestyle for six years, but nothing had clicked spiritually. He decided to meditate under a Bodhi tree and stay in one spot until he found the answer to his search.

The Awakening

During the night, while he slept in the lotus position with his legs crossed, he fought an inner battle with Mara (the personification of change, death, and evil). By morning, Mara was defeated, and Siddhartha awoke with a state of great clarity and understanding of the truth about the way things really are. In his "Awakening," Siddhartha realized that the best spiritual way is a middle path between extremes of self-denial and self-indulgence.

My Name Is Siddhartha Gautama, but My Friends Call Me the Buddha

Siddhartha began to share the message of his awakening—that true knowledge exists between extreme self-indulgence and rigorous self-denial. The people who listened to him sensed a radiance and authority in his message. They gave him the designation of "the Buddha" (which means "the Enlightened One").

Buddha spent the rest of his life teaching his message. He taught and traveled throughout the country until his death at age 80. He died peacefully, with a calm acceptance of death because he knew that he was entering the state of nirvana.

Dr. Hazen Adds...

There are many different versions of the history of the Buddha and the origins of the Buddhist tradition. Written material about Buddha first appears four to six hundred years after his death. There is enough evidence from tradition, late texts, and archaeology to establish that he was a real historical figure. But beyond that we know almost nothing reliable about him, his teaching, and his religious experience.

This Way to the Middle

In his first sermon after the Awakening, Buddha articulated the basic precepts of the enlightenment. The key to living in the "Way of the Middle" between unreasonable excess and unnecessary deprivation is found in Four Noble Truths:

Why Are There So Many Statues of Buddha?

Buddha is not worshiped as a god. However, you might get that impression because there are so many statues of him in Asia and Southeast Asia. Images of Buddha serve as a reminder of the possibility of enlightenment. Buddhists bring offerings of flowers, incense, and light (in the form of burning candles) to the statues in a display of respect.

- **Noble Truth #1:** *Life is all about suffering.* Life is tough. Existence is painful. And because reincarnation keeps the pattern of birth-life-death in a repeating cycle, the suffering doesn't stop with death.

- **Noble Truth #2:** *The cause of suffering is our desire and greed.* There are three root evils: desire, hatred, and ignorance. Our desire and greed is a craving that promotes hatred of others and our ignorance of the true reality. Thus, this selfish craving is at the root of all suffering.

- **Noble Truth #3:** *There is a way to overcome our desire and greed.* The "three fires" of greed, hatred, and ignorance can be "blown out." One can transcend these evils and enter the state of nirvana, and then the cycle of suffering will end.

- **Noble Truth #4:** *The path to happiness and relief of suffering is an eight-step process.* This path is known as the Noble Eightfold Path.

Don't think that the Buddhist religion can be boiled down to just four principles. If you look closely at Noble Truth #4, you'll see that it leads to eight more steps. They are steps of the Noble Eightfold Path, and they involve three qualities:

The *Quality of Wisdom:*
- right understanding (of the world as it really is)
- right thoughts (purifying the mind and heart through thoughts of unselfishness and compassion)

The *Quality of Mental Discipline:*
- right effort (to prevent evil arising within your mind)
- right mindfulness (total attentiveness to the activities of the body, speech, and mind)
- right concentration (training the mind through meditation)

The *Quality of Ethical Conduct:*
- right speech (refraining from lying and any other speech that is hurtful to other people)
- right action (refraining from killing and taking what is not given; avoiding inappropriate sexual conduct, improper speech, and intoxicants)
- right livelihood (earning a living in a way that doesn't bring harm to other people)

This Way to Nirvana

In the next section, we'll discuss two of the major different branches of Buddhism. While there are some distinctions, Buddhists do not usually assert that one path is correct and all others are wrong. (This unusual sense of tolerance even extends to other religions.) For Buddhists, no matter to which branch they belong, it is enough to share the following opinions in common:

- *Samsara:* Life consists of three components: suffering, change, and the absence of an eternal soul that survives independently after death. Buddhists don't consider their personalities to be permanent or individual because they consider each person to be "a flow of being." Everyone is subject to constant physical and psychological change, which continues even after death as the birth process starts its cycle again.

- *Renunciation:* The true reality of life involves the renunciation of life as we know it and believe it to be (before we have attained the dharma of understanding). Without realizing it, we are grasping and craving for a life that doesn't really exist. Only by letting go of it can we obtain the real meaning of life.

- *Reincarnation:* The philosophy that nothing is permanent applies to death. It is just a part of the process of change. What you might consider to be a "person" is just a chain of life. The dead are reborn according to their karma. People are reborn into one of several realms, depending on the progress they made in the last one. The state of mind of a person at the moment of death is important in determining the state of rebirth.

- *Nirvana:* Nirvana is the final state of liberation from the cycle connected to life with suffering. For the most part, it defies description.

- *More Buddhas to come:* Siddhartha Gautama was the first Buddha, but he wasn't the only one. As other people reach the enlightened status, they are Buddhas as well. That is the goal for everyone.

Dr. Hazen Adds…

The key Buddhist teaching of the impermanence (*anitya* in Sanskrit) of all things including the self is displayed in an unusual form of Buddhist art. Monks will spend weeks or months creating intricate and beautiful sand paintings call *mandalas*. They meditate on these for a short period of time and then wipe them out with one motion.

The Three Jewels

There aren't a lot of doctrinal rules and regulations with Buddhism, but there are three fundamental principles upon which the religion is based. These are the *tiratna*, known as the three jewels because they are precious and valuable beliefs:

So Where Does God Fit In?

Buddha wasn't big on God. In fact, while Buddhists aren't opposed to God, they don't consider any deity particularly relevant. After all, divine intervention is not necessary in the process of finding truth and reality through self-introspection. Buddhism is directed toward the spiritual goal that comes through self-discovery and awareness. No importance is placed upon establishing a relationship with God or even becoming aware of God's existence.

- *The first jewel: Buddha.* He found the path of enlightenment and taught it to other people.

- *The second jewel: dharma.* This is the teaching about the true way of things.

- *The third jewel: sangha.* This is the community of monks, nuns, and laypeople who practice and promote the dharma.

It is not uncommon for Buddhists to analogize the three jewels with medical symbolism. For example, Buddha is the physician, the dharma is the remedy, and the sangha is the nurse who administers the remedy.

You can also see the tiratna in Buddhist art. One ancient cloth painting shows Buddha, and above his head is a lotus blossom, representing the teaching of the dharma. Rising out of the flower is a monk to symbolize the sangha.

Sometimes the three jewels are called "the three refuges" because a person who becomes a Buddhist takes refuge from the world around him. A Buddhist chant, repeated three times, goes like this: "I go to the Buddha for refuge; I go to the dharma for refuge; I go to the sangha for refuge."

Dr. Hazen Adds...

The Buddhist tradition has always caused problems for those who wish to come up with an all-encompassing definition of religion. Most definitions want to capture the central idea of humans looking toward a transcendent being or beings. But Buddhism is at its base not only atheistic but nihilistic too. That is, not only does God not exist, but ultimately nothing exists!

What If You Don't Remember Your Past Lives?

Are you skeptical about reincarnation? After all, if you have been born and reborn several times already, how come you don't remember anything from those past lives? According to Buddhist doctrine, only enlightened beings—those who have made it to nirvana—remember their previous lives.

Tibet or Not Tibet? That Is the Question

Few religions are purebreds without any division or differences of opinion or belief in various sects. Buddhism is the same as other religions in this regard, except it has two major traditions. They can be distinguished philosophically, but there also appears to be a geographic dividing line (which makes it a little easier for us to remember).

Buddhists of Tibet

In the regions of Tibet and northern Asia (including China and Japan), the main strain of Buddhism is referred to as *Mahayana*. This tradition includes diverse ways to nirvana and recognizes the important roles of the *bodhisattva*.

Bodhisattva is a term with both a general and a specialized usage. Generally, it means a person who is destined for enlightenment (a person who is a "Buddha to be"). Thus Siddhartha Gautama was a bodhisattva until he actually became the Buddha when he received his Awakening under the Bodhi tree. In a more specialized sense, a bodhisattva is a person who delays entering the nirvana state so that he or she can help other people on the pathway to understanding.

Bodhisattvas follow a path based on six perfections. They will be perfectly...

1. generous
2. virtuous
3. patient

4. energetic

5. meditative

6. wise

The most famous bodhisattva (famous to Buddhists, but probably not famous to you) is Avalokiteshvara, whom Tibetan Buddhists believe is incarnated in the Dalai Lama.

Tibetan Buddhists emphasize the use of the mantra while meditating. *Mantra* means "tool" as in "a tool for meditative thinking" or as "an instrument for the mind." A mantra can be a series of words or a single sound. *Aum* or *Om* are often used for single-sound mantras. Each is repeated frequently throughout the meditation session to invoke a blessing or protection. The number one mantra phrase is *aum mani padme hum* which invokes help from that famous bodhisattva, Avalokiteshvara (who is now famous to even you).

I'm Just Wild About Saffron

A *saffron robe* is that distinctive garment worn by Buddhist monks and nuns. These are hard to miss in a crowd. They are usually some bright shade of orange. They look like bedsheets wrapped around the body in the same manner that fraternity guys would dress for a toga party. Centuries ago the robes were made of discarded rags, but new robes are now given by laypersons to the monks.

Buddhists of Southeast Asia

This branch of the Buddhist family tree is the more conservative and doctrinally strict branch. It is called *Theravada* (meaning "Doctrine of the Elders"), and it is found in the countries of Southeast Asia and in Sri Lanka.

The Theravada focus less on the supreme virtues of a separate life and more on the importance of compassion and service to other people. At the heart of the Theravada is an interdependent relationship between the monks and the laypeople (called "householders"). The laypeople give "offerings" of food and clothes to the monks. They also try to live according to the same moral principles that are binding upon a novice monk. Their acts are motivated out of a desire to become a monk in their next rebirth. (It is unlikely that a layperson will reach nirvana, so hoping for a rebirth as a monk or a nun will get them one step closer.)

Theravada monks live according to the Ten Precepts. The list begins with the same five commitments that apply to laypeople (and novice monks) but adds five more that show the spiritual intensity of life for a monk. A monk (or nun) refrains from these ten things:

1. harming any living thing
2. taking what is not given
3. inappropriate sexual relations
4. wrong speech
5. intoxicating drugs or drink
6. eating after the midday meal
7. dancing, music, singing, and unseemly shows
8. garlands, perfumes, and personal adornments
9. using comfortable chairs or beds
10. accepting gold or silver

The practice of monks is varied. Some live in small groups and do not practice extended meditation because they are involved as spiritual guides and teachers for the villagers. Other monks devote themselves to scholarship or meditation.

Buddhist Vows

A devoted Buddhist will make many vows, including these:
- "Living beings are limitless; I vow to save them."
- "Defilements are inexhaustible; I vow to cut through them."
- "Dharma teachings are immeasurable; I vow to learn them."
- "The Buddha's path is unsurpassable; I vow to realize it and become the Buddha."

Meditate on This

Meditation is the central religious practice for Buddhists. Meditation is the process by which Buddhists pursue the understanding of truth about the nature of reality. It is the means for obtaining dharma.

From the Buddhist perspective, our minds and hearts are like ponds of water that have been stirred up with the activities of our lives and our own greed and cravings. The water is muddy and cloudy as a result of our troubled feelings. Meditation brings stillness that allows the water to settle. Through prolonged meditation, things can clear up so that a person can see deep down within himself and finally gain an understanding about what life really is.

Critics of Buddhist meditation assert that it is an act of mindlessness in which all thoughts are emptied. Such positions misunderstand the principle behind Buddhist meditation. Its goal is complete mindfulness, in which the practitioner is totally aware of the present moment. Yes, for the novice, meditation usually involves sitting in an upright position on the floor in a quiet place to achieve mental calmness. But once the principles of meditation are mastered, it can be practiced while standing, walking, and engaging in the ordinary activities of life.

Meditation should not be considered Buddhism's equivalent of prayer. In other religions, prayer is the conversational process of talking with God and invoking God's involvement in the petitioner's life. Through meditation, however, the Buddhists seek to awaken a source of spiritual power from within themselves (often referred to as "the Buddha-nature within").

We'll End with Zen

Zen isn't the most popular form of Buddhism in the United States, but it gets the most publicity. The word *Zen* roughly means "meditation." This type of Buddhism rejects traditions of form and doctrines and emphasizes instead the realization of one's true self that comes from the personal experience of meditation. In other words, you learn by doing. Don't rely on someone else's teachings or conclusions when you can have a personal experience for yourself instead. The essence of Zen was illustrated by Zen Master Suzuki

Roshi when he was asked to explain the techniques and strategies for *zazen* (sitting meditation). Rather than lecture on the subject, he hopped on a table and sat in silence in the cross-legged position for 30 minutes.

By avoiding intellectual study and relying upon the practice of meditation, it is possible for Zen practitioners to obtain a sudden insight into reality (called a *satori*). In addition to meditating with your legs twisted like a pretzel, Zen employs the use of paradoxical questions (called *koans*) as sort of a shock treatment for the mind. Two of the more famous brain-tweaking koans are:

• What is the sound of one hand clapping?

• What did your face look like before you were born?

The beginnings of Zen Buddhism go back to a guy by the name of Bodhidharma (who was part of the Mahayana school of Buddhism back in the fifth century). It is said that Bodhidharma meditated for nine years straight in order to find personal enlightenment. Afterward he described Zen as...

> a special transmission outside of the scriptures. There was no need for dependence on words and letters; direct pointing to the real person; seeing into one's nature, which was identical with all reality, justified Buddha-life and led to attainment of Buddhahood.

The followers of Bodhidharma emphasize the importance of finding one's own "original mind" and "true nature."

Partly because Zen doesn't depend upon texts or instruction, it survived (and thrived) in China during periods of political and military oppression against religion. But it is not the intent of Zen to make a person self-absorbed or removed from society. Just the opposite. Zen seeks to increase your involvement in the world around you. You can heighten your sensitivity only as you learn to rise above the distractions of worldly delusions (such as anger and illness). Thus, the practice of Zen often includes tranquil activities, such as flower arranging, sweeping leaves, or writing poetry, which can facilitate meditation.

Dr. Hazen Adds...

I have an observation at this point in the book. If you are reading straight through, you have just made a journey from Mormonism to Mahayana Buddhism. These two religions sit on absolute opposite poles of the metaphysical spectrum (remember, metaphysics is what you think is ultimately real). Mormons believe that matter is the only ultimate reality. If something is not material (physical) for the Mormon, it does not exist. On the other end is the philosophically minded Mahayana Buddhist who believes that ultimately nothing exists.

What's That Again?

1. Buddhism got its start in the sixth century BC when Siddhartha Gautama broke away from his isolated, extravagant lifestyle in the palace and was confronted with the harsh realities of real life. For several years he led an austere existence but didn't find satisfaction in that, either.

2. Gautama's great Awakening brought understanding that there is a middle way between the extremes of self-denial and self-indulgence. With this truth, he became the Enlightened One and was thereafter called the Buddha.

3. Buddhists follow the Four Noble Truths that were articulated by Buddha, recognizing that life is all about suffering that is brought about by our own greed and cravings. Suffering can be overcome. By following the Noble Eightfold Path, a person can transcend greed and reach a state of nirvana that is the realization of ultimate truth and understanding.

4. Buddhists believe in reincarnation. Following death, rebirth continues. Ideally, with each rebirth you attain a higher level of understanding until you eventually reach nirvana.

5. Buddhism involves an intense dedication to the practice of meditation. While prayer in other religions is a search to bring God to humanity, the meditation of Buddhists is a search to find the spiritual nature within the individual.

Dig Deeper

Check out *How to Practice: The Way to a Meaningful Life* by His Holiness Dalai Lama (Jeffrey Hopkins, translator). You've heard the expression of "getting it straight from the horse's mouth." Well, that applies here, but we don't mean any disrespect.

Another good introductory resource is *Buddhism Without Beliefs: A Contemporary Guide to Awakening* by Stephen Batchelor.

J. Isamu Yamamoto wrote *Buddhism, Taoism, and Other Far Eastern Religions*. This is like a study guide, and it is written in an outline format. You'll find it particularly helpful if you are trying to compare religions.

We liked Yamamoto's writing style, so we'll also recommend his book *Beyond Buddhism: A Basic Introduction to the Buddhist Tradition*.

$\mathcal{Q}$uestions for $\mathcal{R}$eflection and $\mathcal{D}$iscussion

1. Tell the story of Siddhartha Gautama.

2. What are the principles of the "Way of the Middle"?

3. In what ways do the Four Noble Truths produce a better individual? How do these principles contribute to a better society for all of humanity?

4. If Jesus Christ was having dinner with the Buddha and the conversation turned to theology, what things would they agree about? What would be their points of disagreement?

5. At what point in the reincarnation process will a Buddhist know for certain that his or her faith is true? When is this point of certainty reached for a Christian?

6. Contrast the Ten Commandments with the Ten Precepts. Explain how one is designed to show how we fall short of God's standard, while the other is a checklist for rising to a higher spiritual level.

7. How does Zen meditation differ from the Bible's instruction to meditate on God's Word?

Moving On . . .

Buddhism is prevalent in China, but it wasn't the first major religion there. It didn't arrive in China until it was brought there (probably by traders) in the first and second centuries. For the preceding 700 to 800 years, the Chinese people were following the teachings of Confucius. He is universally recognized as the most influential thinker in Chinese history. He inspired a movement based on modesty, restraint, and respect for rituals. If you think this sounds more like the rules of a social club or some fraternity or sorority, then you have the correct frame of mind to proceed to the next chapter.

Chapter 9

We believe in the formless and eternal Tao,
and we recognize all personified deities
as being mere human constructs. We
reject hatred, intolerance, and unnecessary
violence, and embrace harmony, love
and learning, as we are taught by
Nature. We place our trust and our
lives in the Tao, that we may live in
peace and balance with the Universe,
both in this mortal life and beyond.

Creed of the Western Reform
Taoist Congregation

If there is a grab-bag chapter in this book, this would be it. It's grab-bag in the sense that we are covering three different religions. But these aren't just random "left-over" religions that have nothing in common except our decision to lump them together in chapter 9. These religions have quite a bit in common with each other:

- Each has influenced and is currently followed by millions of people.

- Each originated and remains prevalent in Asia.

- Each is a religion that doesn't always look like a religion.

It's that last point that we think you'll find to be fascinating. Confucianism, for example, might strike you as being more like a philosophy of morality than a religion. Taoism might look like a course listing for Asian social studies with its aspects of art, theater, and fitness. And then there is the Shinto, which adapts so easily to the contemporary culture that it seems almost incompatible with its ancient shrines.

There was another reason that we put these religions together. Over the centuries, they have borrowed principles from each other. They don't seem to be offended by being blended together. If these religions can coexist so compatibly, who are we to separate them?

Eastern Philosophies:
Much More than Just Religious Stuff

𝒲hat's 𝒜head

𝒯he religions we have reviewed to this point all involved allegiance to, or at least entertained the idea of, a god or some other form of deity. Based on reverence or accountability to the divine being, these religions promoted a code of conduct (the "do's and don'ts" of the religion). The religions in this chapter, however, break that trend. God, if there is one, isn't all that important with these religions. And they certainly don't impose rules of behavior according to any deity.

But don't go leaping to the conclusion that these religions give you a loophole for a wild and excessive lifestyle. (Cancel those tickets for Carnival in Rio de Janeiro.) While a god may only play a minor role or none at all in these religions, they are all about ethics, morality, and respect. These religions teach personal responsibility in a context that appears much more *social* than it does *religious*.

Confucianism: It's Not All That Confusing

His real name was K'ung Fu Tzu, but since it is commonly pronounced as Confucius in English, that is what we will call him.

He was born in the middle of the sixth century B.C., in the area of China now known as the Shantung Province. By all accounts, Confucius was a gentle and noble man. Maybe this doesn't surprise you because graciousness is a common trait among Asians. But Confucius was born into a time and culture that was famous for its lack of civility and loose morals.

Confucius was a rebel. That label usually means that a person rejects the customs of his culture. That's exactly what Confucius did. He rejected the immorality of the people around him and blazed a path of morality, integrity, and decency. Confucius believed that resistance to all change was futile, but that his cultural heritage of nobility should not be abandoned by contemporary society; if not kept in check, society would deteriorate into savagery. He considered it his mission to keep alive the idea of dignified and gracious conduct. Much of his life was spent traveling throughout the country, advising rulers on ethical standards of governance.

---

*U*ntil you know about life, how can you know about death?

Confucius

Can You Relate to This?

Confucianism essentially focuses on the question of the ultimate meaning of life. In that regard, a Confucian is always considering questions like these:

- What makes life worth living?

- What are the virtues and methods of self-discipline needed to create an existence worthy of esteem?

Did you notice something curiously missing from those questions? It is *God*. Confucianism doesn't have a lot of doctrines about God that are common to other religions. It is primarily a belief system of ethical behavior that people should use in their relationships with each other. Sometimes those relationships are on the macro level (such as how governments should treat their citizens); other times those relationships are at the micro level (such as one-to-one personal interaction).

Confucius taught that the most meaningful parts of life are found in five ethical relationships:

1. the parent-child relationship

2. the relationship between rulers and their subjects

3. the husband-wife relationship

4. the relationship between siblings

5. the relationship between friends

You can see why Confucianism has universal appeal. You probably have relationships that fall into several of those categories.

Dr. Hazen Adds...

The practical wisdom of Confucius found in his famous proverbs is profound. Indeed, many of his proverbs parallel the practical wisdom found in the book of Proverbs in the Bible—but with one important difference. At the beginning of the book of Proverbs, the Bible recognizes that the beginning of wisdom is to understand that God exists and that we should revere Him first. And this makes perfect sense. If God does in fact exist and hold our destiny in His hand, how can one possibly be considered wise and not recognize that?

But just being in one of the valuable relationships won't make your life tranquil. You can probably attest to that fact. Hey, one or more of those relationships is probably causing you considerable grief in your life. That's where the teachings of Confucius become important. He emphasized certain ethical values that should be personally applied in the important relationships of life:

- *Li*: proper conduct and etiquette

- *Hsiao*: love between family members

- *Yi*: righteousness, decency, and virtue

- *Xin*: honesty and trustworthiness

- *Jen*: kindness towards others

- *Chung*: loyalty and faithfulness

These values are almost universally appreciated by people everywhere, even those who are adherents of other religions. Consequently, in China and other parts of Asia, the teachings of Confucius are often blended with other religions. For example, Confucian thought is often combined with the Taoists' worship of nature, or with the concepts of the afterlife held by Buddhists.

A Quick Look at Eastern Philosophies

- There are approximately six million Confucians in the world. About 26,000 live in North America; almost all of the remainder are found throughout China and the rest of Asia.

- Taoism currently has about 20 million followers and is primarily centered in Taiwan. About 30,000 Taoists live in North America.

- Taoism has had a significant influence on North American culture in areas of acupuncture, herbal medicine, and the martial arts.

- As the next few sentences will reveal, statistics on the numbers of adherents in a religion are hopelessly unreliable. One source puts the number of worldwide Shinto followers in the range of 2.8 to 3.2 million. Another source states that 40 percent of Japanese adults follow Shinto (which would mean there are about 50 million adherents). A different source states that about 86 percent of Japanese adults follow a combination of Shinto and Buddhism (which would put the number of followers of Shinto at 107 million).

- Unlike most other religions, Shinto has no real founder, no written scriptures, no body of religious law, and only a very loosely organized priesthood.

- In Japan, there are about 80,000 shrines to honor the gods *(kami)* of Shinto.

Worthy to Be Read

The core principles of Confucianism are contained in nine books. (This might seem like a lot, but don't forget that the Bible is actually a composite of 66 books.) The books were individually written, but they were categorized and assembled in the twelfth century (during the Sung dynasty) into two sets:

The Five Classics: These books were supposedly written before Confucius's time:

1. the *Shi Jing:* an anthology of 300 poems and songs

2. the *Shu Jing:* a collection of historical documents attributed to the legendary and early rulers in China

3. the *Li Ji:* a collection of writings relating to rituals

4. the *Chun Qui:* a historical account of the Lu, the home region of Confucius

5. the *I Ching*: a collection of 64 hexagrams (symbols composed of broken and continuous lines) with specified meanings

The Four Books: These books contain the writings of Confucius and Mencius (one of the leading followers of Confucianism whom we will mention below):

1. The *Lun Yu:* Often called the Analects, it contains a record of the deeds and sayings of Confucius.

2. The *Chung Yung:* It is called "The Doctrine of the Mean" (whatever that means).

3. The *Ta Hsueh:* It is referred to as the Book of Great Learning.

4. The *Meng Tzu:* These are the writings of Mencius who, like Confucius, traveled from state to state advising rulers on proper conduct and governance.

Of all of these books, the one that holds the most fascination for people of the Western culture is the *I Ching*. Tradition holds that Confucius wrote the commentaries for the meanings of the hexagrams. The *I Ching* (called the Book of Changes) is considered a manual to obtain guidance for decisions in life. The book is used with 49 sticks (like skinny chopsticks) that are tossed on the ground. The random pattern of sticks determines which hexagram should be referenced for the answer to the question. (It is a bit like the ancient Asian equivalent of the magic eight ball.)

Changing the Cultural Perspective

Confucius was born in the midst of China's great dynasties. He was born into an upper-class family just as the aristocracies were giving way to larger new monarchies governed by men without strong family traditions. The reverence of wisdom was being replaced with a devotion to wealth, and oppression of the poor was growing more commonplace. Confucius believed that society as a whole was a reflection of the character of the ruling class. He believed that the character of the ruler influenced the nature of the individual subjects. Bucking the cultural trend, Confucius taught that if a ruler was good and fair, then the people in his kingdom would be honest and submissive; conversely, a cruel and demanding ruler would produce contentious and selfish citizens. Although his message was not popular with the ruling class at the time he preached it, the message took hold over the centuries and changed the course of Chinese society.

The influence of Confucianism has permeated Chinese culture ever since, despite oppressive political and military regimes that have been in power from time to time over the centuries. Communist governments have attempted to oppress the teachings of Confucius, but his ethical principles still find expression in the heart of many of the Chinese people (and influence their opinion of the ruling authorities).

Inherently Good or Inherently Bad?

The teaching of Confucius spread rapidly after his death. Although he was involved in the writing of several books to preserve his teachings, apparently he didn't write enough. There was room enough for some major ambiguity to arise several hundred years after his death. The practical concerns for conduct were taken to an intellectual level in two opposing schools of thought (identified by their original proponents). Both branches continued to acknowledge the importance of appropriate behavior, but they disagreed upon how to determine what is appropriate:

- *Mencius (c. 371–289 B.C.):* This guy believed that people are inherently good, so their intuition can be the guide for appropriate behavior. He is famous for his theory that the "seeds" of goodness exist naturally in everyone but have to be carefully nurtured if they are ever to grow and develop. He also believed that government should be structured to allow the "good" of the majority to prevail in order to produce a "benevolent government." (He is recognized as one of the early advocates of democracy.)

- *Xunzi (c. 300–230 B.C.):* This guy's opinion was just the opposite. He believed that humans are born with an innately evil nature. They must have a rigid system of specified *Li* (conduct and etiquette) in order to become virtuous. Thus, Xunzi was more concerned with preventing behavior that was morally unacceptable. He didn't view the imposition of established codes of conduct to be punitive; rather, he believed that they were worthy in and of themselves because they brought people from bad to good.

Although there was never really a contest between them, the views of Mencius have seemed to prevail. Traditional Confucianism adopts his belief that each person has the potential for realizing the four virtues of humanity, righteousness, propriety, and wisdom. His views, which represent the essence of Confucianism, are summarized in his statement:

> All things are within me, and on self-examination, I find no greater joy than to be true to myself. We should do our best to treat others as we wish to be treated. Nothing is more appropriate than to seek after goodness.

Through the centuries since Mencius, Confucianism has undergone further refinements, alterations, and adjustments (with movements known as neo-Confucianism and contemporary neo-Confucianism). There have even been hybrid forms along geopolitical boundaries (such as Korean Confucianism, Japanese Confucianism, and Singaporean Confucianism). Despite these variations, Confucianism remains today as it was originally articulated by Confucius himself: a system of thought by which cordial and civilized behavior is emphasized for the benefit of life's most important relationships.

Taoism: Nature Is a Big Mother

We are going to leave Confucianism for a while, but we aren't going to go too far away from it. We are moving on to Taoism. *Daoism* is the more current term, but *Taoism* is more frequently used in the Western world, so that is the one we'll stick with. (The change seems a bit senseless when you learn that *Tao* is pronounced as "dow," so it doesn't seem to matter whether the word starts with a *T* or a *D*.)

Taoism is closely related to Confucianism. They have coexisted for centuries in the same geographical region and often within the same followers. Taoism's greatest difference with Confucianism has to do with philosophy, and the two aren't all that different there, either. While Confucianism is focused on morality and civility within the society, Tao is more concerned with the world of nature. The rough English translation of *Tao* means "the way," as in "the way of nature."

Defining the Indefinable

When asked to explain their beliefs, followers of the Tao state that it is basically indefinable. That didn't stop us. In our research (obviously obtained from people who didn't know enough about Taoism to know that it is indefinable), the Tao has been described as...

- a power that envelops, surrounds, and flows through all things, living and nonliving
- the energy that regulates natural processes and nourishes balance in the universe
- the force that brings harmony to opposites (such that there would be no love without hate, no light without dark, and no male without female)
- the first cause of the universe

The Yin and Yang of It

You can't understand the Eastern philosophies without knowing about *yin* and *yang*. No, these are not two panda bears at the Beijing Zoo. Yin and yang represent the interrelated and offsetting principles of consistency and change.

Eastern philosophies are based on the concepts of continuity and change. While these may seem like opposite notions to you, the Asian cultures have understood the importance of their connectedness. On one hand, Asian cultures revere their link to the past (including their ancestors and culture); conversely, they also appreciate the flexibility and change that occurs in life. Instead of competing with each other, these two concepts can be blended and balanced to produce harmony in life.

Yin and yang are the polar opposites that produce energy for life. The universe is seen as existing in a state of this binary division of opposing but complementary natural principles. For everything there is a yin side (dark, soft, and feminine), and a yang counterpart (bright, hard, and masculine). This produces the differences between male and female, day and night, joy and sorrow. By understanding the "correlative thinking" of the yin and yang, you can attain balance in your life no matter what circumstances come your way.

Yin and yang are typically symbolized by a circle divided into two halves (each half in a swirl the shape of a pollywog). One half is white and the other half is black, with a dot of the opposite color in each swirl.

Upon this foundation of the importance of nature, Taoism adds a philosophy of the importance of each individual. (Hey, why not? We are all a part of nature.) Just as nature should be allowed to follow its own course, so should individuals be allowed to follow their own inclinations, free from restrictions imposed by other people. Similar to the Confucian views of Mencius, Taoists believe that people are compassionate by nature and that they will show compassion to others (without any expectation of reward) if they are left to their own natural instincts.

A Laozi Way to Start the Tao

The founder of Taoism is generally believed to be Laozi. He was a contemporary of Confucius who lived in the sixth century B.C. He was worried that brutality upon the masses was on the increase as local rulers struggled to conquer their neighboring opponents. Thus, he emphasized the importance of each individual as an important component within the world of nature.

Laozi is credited with writing the *Daodejing*, one of the revered texts of Taoism that contains pithy philosophical sayings. The story is told that Laozi was a historian in charge of the ancestral archives in his province of Zhou. When he recognized that the society around him was deteriorating, he rode on an ox to escape to the mountains in the west. At a mountain pass, he was confronted by the mystical "guardians of the frontier," who asked him to write down his wisdom and teachings. It was at that point that he penned a book, the *Daodejing*, in a total of 5000 characters, setting down the ideas of the Tao. As soon as he was finished, he vanished into thin air and was never heard from again. All that remained behind was the *Daodejing* (and, we are guessing, the ox).

While Taoism may have started as a combination of psychology and philosophy with Laozi, it evolved into a religious faith by the fifth century A.D. when it was adopted as a state religion. By that time, Laozi was revered as a deity.

Taoism eventually became one of the great religions of China (along with Buddhism and Confucianism). It was an official state religion until the end of the Ch'ing Dynasty in 1911, when governmental support of Taoism terminated. In the following period of the warlords, many of the Taoist temples and artifacts were destroyed. The situation got even worse after the Communist victory in 1949 when even less religious freedom was allowed and the Communist government confiscated temples and plundered religious memorials. The final blow to much of the Taoist heritage was dealt during the Cultural Revolution in China from 1966 to 1976. The current regime of Chinese government has permitted the people to return to the outward expression of their Taoist beliefs.

Doing What Comes Naturally

The combination of Tao's emphasis on the energy of nature and the importance of the individual produces some interesting aspects to its philosophy. Consider these:

- Spontaneous action *(wu wei)* is emphasized. This applies not only on the personal level but also with respect to nature. Since nature should be allowed to "take its own course," no one should erect a dam that would impede a river's natural flow towards the sea.

- All value judgments are relative.

- Each believer's goal is to become one with the Tao.

- Time is cyclical, not linear as in Western thinking.

The popularity of Taoism in the United States is related to its emphasis on health and fitness. But this isn't health and fitness of the Gold's Gym variety. It involves a holistic approach to wellness, involving acupuncture, herbal medicine, and meditation. And while much of America is caught up in the frenzied pace of aerobics, followers of the Tao go through the same motions, only in slow motion with the ancient techniques of *tai chi*. The slow, choreographed movements of tai chi exercise all parts of the body. It is designed to stimulate the central nervous system while lowering blood pressure and relieving stress. It gently tones muscles without straining them. Tai chi also enhances digestion, the elimination of wastes, and the circulation of blood. Traditional Chinese medicine teaches that illness is caused by blockages or a lack of balance in the body's *chi* (intrinsic energy). Tai chi is believed to restore the necessary balance of this energy flow. We like to think of tai chi as a massage of your internal organs. (It may be slow, but it is better than touching them.)

Dr. Hazen Adds...

*A*nother ancient practice deeply rooted in Taoist ideas of balance and harmony is one we are hearing more and more about today. *Feng shui*, the art of creating a balanced living environment—especially in architectural design and furniture arrangement—has become immensely popular on the West Coast of the United States.

I'm Gonna Live Forever

During the second century B.C., when Taoism was only a few hundred years old, its followers believed that it was possible to find an elixir in nature that would confer immortality on them. Unfortunately, cinnabar was the main ingredient in the supposed potion, and it is highly poisonous; consequently, many people died in their quest for immortality. These frequent fatalities caused Taoists to alter their quest a bit. Instead of looking for physical immortality, they tried the safer route of looking for an inner philosophical potion that would give them an "immortal embryo" that could be achieved by mental and physical disciplines. (The movements of tai chi were much safer than drinking poison.)

This shift from a quest for physical immortality to a search for inner immortality led to the concept of *qi* (which means "breath"). Qi is the primal energy that Taoists believe flows through the body, as well as through the entire universe. You can learn to control the qi through tai chi exercises. It was originally believed that bodily control of the qi in certain sexual practices could result in immortality. One ancient text indicates that a man could achieve 10,000 years of life if he could sustain sexual encounters with 108 women; permanent immortality would require no fewer than 1200 women. (We are sure that it was a *guy* who came up with this theory.)

---

*B*e still like a mountain and flow like a great river.

Laozi

Shinto: Into the Here and Now

Shinto began in Japan about 500 B.C. or earlier as an unstructured mixture of nature worship, fertility cults, and divination techniques. In its earliest forms it was centered in *kami* (the belief that gods inhabited the mountains, trees, rocks, and other objects of nature). By the sixth century A.D., kami was blended with aspects of Buddhism, Confucianism, and Taoism that had come to Japan from China. The result of this philosophical fusion by the eighth century A.D. was the religion of Shinto, a name derived from the Chinese words *shin tao* ("the way of the gods").

Shinto has always consisted of two interdependent traditions— a popular side and a political side:

- *The popular side of Shinto:* In every neighborhood and village there are kami shrines, so it is entrenched in the Japanese culture at the local, populous level.

- *The political side of Shinto:* The rituals and priests of Shinto have been integrated into the political structure to the point where they legitimized Japanese rulers. From the time of the new Meiji emperor in 1868 until 1945, Shinto became the state religion of Japan and was used to promote Japan's imperialistic ideology. After World War II, the government structure was disengaged from its connection with Shinto when the emperor renounced his divinity.

Today, free of any forced connection with the government, Shinto represents a form of nature worship, recognizing the presence of kami within all aspects of nature.

---

*O*rigami, that Japanese art of folding paper, has religious significance. It comes out of the Shinto experience. *Origami* means "paper of the spirits," and the beautiful paper figures often decorate Shinto shrines. Because paper comes from trees, and because a spirit is within the paper, origami paper is never cut, only folded.

The Affirmations

As you're about to see, Shinto is heavy on ritual but light on doctrine. While there isn't a lot of theology in this religion, it does have four "affirmations" that stand for common beliefs that followers of Shinto "agree are good":

1. *Tradition and the family:* The family is seen as the primary institution by which traditions are preserved. It is through the family that heritage and traditions are passed from one generation to the next. The sense and importance of the family is celebrated on the occasions of births and marriages.

2. *Love of nature:* Nature is sacred. If you are close to nature, then you are close to kami (the gods of nature). The objects in nature should be worshiped as sacred spirits.

3. *Physical cleanliness:* A respect for nature demands cleanliness. This is not just a ceremonial cleanliness at the time of rituals; it applies all of the time. Bathing and washing hands is required because you are constantly in contact with the surroundings of nature.

4. *"Matsuri":* These are festivals in honor of one or more of the kami and ancestral spirits. The Matsuri promote community unity by creating an opportunity for family and friends to socialize with each other.

It Is a Religion; It's Not a Religion

The central focus of Shinto is the kami (gods) within the world. But for followers of Shinto, the "world" is the here and now and not some metaphysical other dimension that involves the afterlife or eternity. Since the kami are present in nature, there is virtually no concern with heaven. Thus, while Shinto has many of the trappings of a religion, there are many aspects of it that suggest that it is not a religion (at least not a religion in the normal sense of that word).

An Ancient Religion That's Good for Today

For an ancient religion (perhaps the oldest in Japan, if you go back to the pre-Shinto days of the kami cult), Shinto translates well into contemporary Japanese culture. This is due, in part, to the fact that Shinto focuses on the present world. Since it doesn't get

Shinto

It Is a Religion	It Is Not a Religion
Shinto has lots of gods.	It has no concept of a divine Creator.
Shinto has priests.	It has no founder or patriarchs.
Shinto has lots of rituals.	It has no particular ethical system.
Shinto has an abundance of shrines.	It has no sacred texts.
Shinto stresses participation.	It does not emphasize belief.
At some point in their lives, 95 percent of Japanese people go to a Shinto shrine.	Only 20 percent of Japanese people who participate actually believe in the existence of the kami.
Shinto believes that kami (gods) inhabit all objects of nature.	There is no particular belief that humans have a "soul" or eternal nature.

bogged down with doctrine of an afterlife, everything revolves around what is happening now. Furthermore, since there are innumerable kami that exist in all aspects of nature, it is easy for Shinto to blend into the fabric of modern Japanese society. Although it has some of the frills that accompany traditional religions (such as priests, temples, and rituals), those have blended into secular society more as contemporary routine than as sacred religion.

The kami adapt to cultural changes as well. They are shadowy beings—not usually personified in form or personality—that possess supernatural power to affect the objects that they inhabit. For centuries, *Inari* (the kami "Rice Provider") has been the most popular. Thirty thousand shrines are dedicated to Inari. While

The Beliefs of Eastern Philosophies

What About...   **According to Eastern Philosophies...**

God
While gods may play a part in the philosophy (such as the Shinto kami), they are not the focal point. Human behavior plays a more important role than the involvement of any god.

Humanity
Humanity is generally viewed as good and noble. If allowed to follow natural instincts (free from the oppression of government), people will show kindness and respect to each other.

Sin
There are acceptable and unacceptable forms of behavior. Violation of the codes of ethical conduct can be pardoned by repentance and resuming proper behavior.

Salvation and the Afterlife
There is not really an afterlife, but there is the concept of nirvana, which is a level of ultimate knowledge and understanding. There is no concept of salvation by a god. You reach nirvana by attaining progressively higher levels of knowledge through your various life cycles.

Morals
Moral behavior is the most important thing of life.

Worship
While there is ritual worship of gods, there is no concept of committing one's self to God. Even members of the priesthood have a devotion to community and humanity that seems to overshadow a devotion to God.

Jesus
There is no acknowledgment or recognition of Jesus other than as a person who lived and taught moral conduct that was consistent with the teachings of the Eastern philosophies.

Shinto is essentially indigenous and exclusive to Japan. It is difficult for someone outside of Japan (or without Japanese ancestry) to embrace Shinto. Since there is no Bible-like text from which a person can learn about the religion, Shinto must be learned by experiencing the rituals. Shinto primarily passes down from one generation to the next by practicing the rituals as a group.

originally just a guardian kami of agriculture, Inari's job duties expanded during the industrial and technological revolutions in Japan. Today, Inari is petitioned to act on behalf of a wide variety of businesses and commerce.

It is not uncommon to find Shinto priests performing rites to invoke a kami to pacify the earth for a blessing on a construction company or for blessings on a new car. Businessmen pray to the kami for good returns on the Nikki Index (the Japanese stock market), and students pray to the kami for success in exams.

What's That Again?

1. Confucius was the founder of a system of thought that emphasizes moral and virtuous behavior.

2. Confucianism values the relationships of husbands and wives, parents and children, siblings, friends, and the government and its citizens. Within these relationships, people should exhibit love to each other, loyalty, manners, honesty, decency, and kindness.

3. Taoism reveres and worships the power and energy force that is within nature.

4. While Confucianism emphasizes the importance of community relationships, Taoism focuses on the significance of the individual. Each person is a part of nature, so each person experiences the Tao. The trick is to control and harness the Tao within to its maximum advantage (and the movement techniques of tai chi are used for this purpose).

5. Shinto focuses on the here and now. With no particular belief in an afterlife, the present world becomes the primary emphasis.

6. Shinto gods (kami) are in all of nature. The ritual practices of worship to these gods is more important than an actual belief in them.

Dig Deeper

An excellent guide to Eastern religions and philosophies is *The Perennial Dictionary of World Religions* (Harper & Row, originally published as *Abingdon's Dictionary of Living Religions*). It gives a good overview of all of the basic concepts for each belief system.

If you are looking for an in-depth resource on Confucianism, you might want to check out *Confucius and the Chinese Way* by H.G. Creel. As the title indicates, the emphasis is on the practice of Confucianism within China, but the variant forms in other countries are not much different.

If you want an Internet Tao resource, go to www.taoresource.com (clever, huh?). This is a website that imports authentic Taoist products to help people improve their "personal or sacred space, to build a small Taoist shrine, or even to construct a large Taoist temple."

Sokyo Ono is a top Shinto scholar, and he gives an excellent introduction to Shinto's spiritual characteristics and its influences on Japanese culture in his book *Shinto: The Kami Way.*

■ ■ ■

Questions for Reflection and Discussion

1. Describe Confucianism in a single sentence.

2. Even though they are similar at points, what are the biggest differences between the proverbs of Confucius and the proverbs of the Bible?

3. What are some teachings of Confucius that a Christian might embrace?

4. Explain how Confucianism has been able to survive in Chinese culture despite periods of political oppression.

5. Read the statement that summarizes the views of Mencius. Is there anything wrong with this statement? Do you agree or disagree with the belief of traditional Confucianism that every person has the potential for realizing the four virtues of humanity, righteousness, propriety, and wisdom. Why or why not?

6. In what ways has Taoism become a part of Western culture? Give two examples.

7. Explain why the ancient beliefs of Shinto translate well into contemporary Japanese culture.

Moving On . . .

As you have seen, God plays a relatively minor role in the philosophical religions. He is there, but He doesn't matter very much. We are about to take one step further away from God. In part 4, we get to religions that have no God at all. Some of them even go beyond "no god" to the point of being "anti-god."

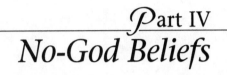

*P*art IV
No-God Beliefs

Chapter 10

The certain test of sanity is
if you accept life whole, as it is.

Laozi

As we began our study of New Age spirituality, we weren't sure we would be able to find enough material to fill an entire chapter. We thought the New Age movement had died with the Age of Aquarius and the hippie era of the 1960s. Boy, were we wrong. As we did our research, not only did we learn that the New Age movement is alive and well, but we also discovered that it just might be the most widespread and influential spiritual belief system of the twenty-first century.

At the dawning of the New Age movement, people were talking and singing about rather bizarre concepts, such as...

- mystic crystal revelations
- the planets aligning to produce harmony of the inner spirit
- liberation of the mind achieved through holistic tranquility

A generation ago, most people considered the New Age a fad because it seemed so quirky. The Nehru jackets may have faded away, but New Age beliefs have remained and flourished.

So get out your love beads and lava lamp. It's time to dig into the New Age.

New Age Spirituality:
A Little of This and a Little of That

*T*he onion is one of nature's most unusual foods. It isn't too impressive until you smell it or take a bite, and then the pungent flavor hits you like a...well, like an onion (and then you need a breath mint). As we begin this chapter, we want to make a comparison between the qualities of the onion and New Age spirituality:

- It grows below ground.
- It has many layers.
- It's strong-smelling.
- It can make you cry.

Like the lowly onion, the New Age movement has been largely underground and undetected—until now. With the dawning of a new millennium has come the dawning of a New Age. Rather than sit on the sidelines, millions of New Age advocates and practitioners now believe it's time to actively bring about a new era of self-discovery, spiritual awareness, personal enlightenment, and global unity. New Age spirituality is hard to pin down because there are many layers embedded in all aspects of society—health care, business, science, politics, sports, and entertainment. But the influence of New Age beliefs is there, and it's growing. In case you haven't noticed, New Age spirituality is impacting the world—especially America—as strongly as a raw onion flavors a hamburger.

It's Not a Conspiracy

If we sound like alarmists, we don't mean to be. We don't believe that there's a vast New Age conspiracy threatening to take over the world. But we do believe—and the evidence shows—that there are millions of well-educated, articulate, influential professionals who are committed to practicing and teaching New Age spirituality to tens of millions of other people through books, tapes, seminars, television shows, and websites. On the fringes (the outer layers of the onion) some of the New Age spirituality sounds a lot like Christianity (and, in fact, many Christians are attracted to New Age teaching). There's an emphasis on healthful living, inner peace, harmony with other human beings, respect for the planet, and integrity. But at its core, New Age spirituality is radically different than biblical Christianity.

Why Do They Call It the New Age?

The term *New Age*, which has been around for at least 50 years, is a utopian vision that describes a new era of harmony and human progress. The Age of Aquarius is tied to the eleventh sign of the zodiac. According to astrologers, Aquarians are visionary, open-minded, individualistic, and eccentric.

Our goal is to open your eyes to this giant onion called New Age spirituality. We're going to peel back the outer layers so you can see it the way New Age advocate David Spangler describes it in his book *Revelation: The Birth of a New Age*:

> The New Age is a concept that proclaims a new opportunity, a new level of growth attained, a new power

released and at work in human affairs, a new manifestation of that evolutionary tide of events which, taken at the flood, does indeed lead on to greater things, in this case to a new heaven, a new earth, and a new humanity.

The Corporate Mystic

Our search for the meaning of New Age spirituality began at our neighborhood Starbucks, where we do a lot of our research. We were there to talk about this chapter (and to drink coffee, of course), when we happened to observe a well-dressed businessman reading a book entitled *The Corporate Mystic*. We didn't think that mystics were corporate types, so we decided to find out what this book was all about. The corporate guy finished his coffee and left before we had a chance to ask him directly, so we had to find the book for ourselves.

That wasn't too difficult. Our local Barnes & Noble bookstore has a rather large section of books devoted to New Age spirituality, and without any trouble we found the book, written by a psychotherapist by the name of Gay Hendricks. We had never heard of him, but apparently some well-known corporate heavyweights believe that Dr. Hendricks offers "a unique and thought-provoking perspective on management and leadership." It didn't take us long to find out that Dr. Hendricks' perspective is rooted in mysticism and intuition rather than objective business principles. Dr. Stephen Covey, whose books have been studied by church and business leaders alike, endorses *The Corporate Mystic* as a book that will "sweep you into a different level of consciousness—one of spiritual perspective and feeling."

We wondered, "Is this the direction the corporate world is taking?" The publisher of *The Corporate Mystic* certainly thinks so: "If you want to find a genuine mystic, you are more likely to find one in a boardroom than a monastery or a cathedral."

---

*T*he Encarta World English Dictionary defines *mysticism* as "the belief that personal communication or union with the divine is achieved through faith, ecstasy, or sudden insight rather than through rational thought."

A Quick Look at New Age Spirituality

- According to Russell Chandler, "New Age is not a cult or a sect, per se," but rather "a hybrid mix of spiritual, social, and political forces, and it encompasses sociology, theology, the physical sciences, medicine, anthropology, history, the human potential movement, sports, and science fiction."

- As many as 12 million Americans are active New Age participants.

- Another 30 million are "avidly interested."

- There is no definitive statement of New Age beliefs, no founder, no central church or headquarters, and no formal structure.

- More than 3000 publishers offer New Age and occult books.

- Bestselling New Age books include *A Course in Miracles*, *A Return to Love*, *Out on a Limb*, and *The Celestine Prophecy*.

Breathwork and Movement

We decided to dig further, so we checked the Internet (www.hen dricks.com) for information on the Hendricks Institute, an international learning center founded by Dr. Hendricks and his wife that teaches "Core Skills for Conscious Living." At the time we checked, the institute was featuring the "Center for Professional Breathwork and Movement," a course designed to bring "somatic transformation to the mainstream in health, business, sports, and other fields." As we searched the website, we found many recurring words and phrases that were best summed up by the renowned New Age spiritualist, Dr. Deepak Chopra:

> The inner intelligence of the body is the ultimate and supreme genius. Gay and Kathlyn Hendricks show us how to connect with this inner intelligence and

discover the secrets to healing, love, intuition, and insight.

Now we don't mean to pick on Dr. Hendricks. From all outward appearances, he and his wife seem like very nice, very competent, very sincere people. Their faculty of trainers includes several psychotherapists and medical doctors (Dr. Hendricks himself has serious credentials and has taught at Stanford University and the University of Colorado). Our point is to show you that Dr. Hendricks is just one of many nice, competent, sincere, and capable people who are doing their best to call out a "new type of professional in the twenty-first century."

Somatic: Relating or affecting the body as considered separate from the mind.

Total Transformation

Just who are these professionals? We found another book that gave us plenty of answers. *Imagine What America Could Be in the 21st Century* is more than a book with a long title. Edited by Marianne Williamson, an Oprah regular and the author of the number one *New York Times* bestseller *A Return to Love,* the book includes "Visions of a Better Future" from "leading American thinkers."

We recognized many of the contributors, such as Anne Lamott, a spiritual writer who has a following among many thoughtful and serious Christians. She believes these professionals are scientists, philosophers, and storytellers. "They have visions, they have dreams, and they also have schemes and plans for implementing their visions." Neale Donald Walsh, author of *Conversations with God,* is more direct about what he sees in the twenty-first century: "Total transformation. That's what I see in America by the middle of this century.... Our experience will be one of unity *because we will all come to know the same thing at the same time.*"

James Redfield, author of the number one *New York Times* bestseller *The Celestine Prophecy,* writes:

> In this new worldview of ours, I believe we are becoming even more centered on what we must do

next. We must push even further, knock on the door with more intention, open up more fully to the mysteries surrounding our lives. We must open up to a greater, spiritual side of ourselves that all the mystics declare is waiting.

Thomas Moore, a former Catholic monk who wrote the bestseller *Care of the Soul,* believes that "for many, religion is definitely out while spirituality is in." He observes: "People are meditating, eating differently, forming new churches and communities, and looking for Indian gurus and Sufi poets for inspiration."

All About the Onion

The more we investigated, the more we saw a pattern that included words and concepts like *intuition, transformation, self-awareness, body-wisdom, enlightenment,* and *divine intelligence.* Is this what New Age spirituality is all about, and if so, what does it mean? To make sure we were barking up the right tree, we asked our adviser, Dr. Craig Hazen, to give us a handle on the New Age movement. Dr. Hazen received his doctorate in comparative religion from the University of California at Santa Barbara, which has one of the leading religious studies programs in the nation. Here's what he told us:

Dr. Hazen Adds...

*T*he terms you mention do have something important in common that I believe characterizes much of what the New Age stands for: inwardness. New Age beliefs have been described as "intense navel gazing" because people are encouraged to discover the truth almost exclusively inside themselves. Traditional religions certainly have an inward dimension to them, but they almost all start with looking outside of one's self for revelation from above, or to nature, or to wise teachers for spiritual enlightenment.

Dr. Ron Rhodes lists several characteristics of the New Age movement. Since there's no central authority or set of beliefs, he's not saying that every New Age practitioner would agree with everything on this list. But taken as a whole, these characteristics pretty much encompass the basic New Age beliefs:

- *Religious syncretism*—Syncretism happens when you combine different systems of religious and philosophical beliefs and practices (even if they contradict each other). This is very big with New Age spiritualists. They are comfortable with many Christian beliefs, but they also embrace ancient Hinduism, Native American practices, and psychic phenomenon.

- *Monism*—We have already defined *monism* as "all is one." Many New Agers see all reality as a "unified whole." This is what Neale Donald Walsh means by "true unity" and knowing "the same thing at the same time." When Dr. Hendricks teaches "conscious living," he refers to an aspect of monism whereby all people tap into the same awareness and grand consciousness of life.

- *Pantheism*—This is the belief that "all is God" and "God is all." All reality is divine. Thomas Moore writes, "Religion is a method of connecting to the mysteries that we find in our world and in ourselves." James Redfield writes about moving toward a "completely spiritual culture on Earth" by unlocking the insights in each human being.

- *Deification of humanity*—Since God is in everything, then human beings are divine or at least capable of becoming like God. One of the hottest topics in the corporate seminar world is the "human potential movement." Dr. Hendricks teaches, "The Corporate Mystic knows that real power and real fun come from being a source. When you are the source, you take full responsibility for bringing into being the corporate culture you want. Everyone can be the source, and when they think they are, they are."

- *Transformation*—We kept running into the word *transformation*. It didn't sound so bad. Even the Bible talks about letting God "transform you into a new person by changing the way you think" (Romans 12:2). Except that's not what it means to New Age spiritualists. For one thing, the idea of a personal God doing the transformation doesn't enter into the equation, and for another, they have a very different understanding of transformation. Dr. Rhodes explains, "Personal transformation hinges on one's personal recognition of oneness with God, humanity, and the universe." This "recognition" is equated with "enlightenment" or "self-actualization." In other words, it's human centered, not God-centered.

Then there is *planetary* transformation, which has nothing to do with traveling to other planets, and everything to do with transforming our own planet into a new world by uniting as one in consciousness and insight.

- *Ecological centeredness*—According to the biblical perspective, the human race was given a mandate to manage and care for the earth shortly after God finished His work of creation (Genesis 1:26-28). But the New Agers go way beyond management to reverence and, in some cases, worship. The philosophy of monism opens the door for this perspective. Since everything is part of one reality, then we are related to the earth. Anne Lamott writes that we need to "love the planet back to health: to feed her, care for her, esteem her people, and heal the decades of abuse we've heaped upon her."

- *Belief in a new world order*—The whole idea of a coming utopia is nothing new (actually, nothing in New Age spirituality is new, as we're going to discover shortly). What is new is that leading New Age thinkers are openly calling for a new world order featuring a one-world government and a unified global society in which all people are one through their common spiritual beliefs and consciousness. Many New Agers are hopeful that this will occur by the middle of this century.

We want to emphasize again that the New Age spiritualists we studied aren't members of your garden-variety cult. These aren't people who would line up behind some kook who's offering to transport them to another planet. As we said, New Age teachers and practitioners are thoughtful, intelligent, passionate people who want nothing more than for their fellow human beings to get along with each other and have respect for the earth. They are well-educated, successful, spiritually centered, and open-minded people. But what is the source of what they believe? In order to answer that question, we need to examine the soil where this New Age onion has put down roots. We need to find out where the New Age beliefs came from.

Do New Agers Believe in Reincarnation?

It wasn't too long ago that many people were all laughing at Shirley MacLaine, whose book *Out on a Limb* exposed her belief in reincarnation. Nobody's laughing now, because her ideas have become a part of mainstream New Age thinking (surveys show that 30 million Americans believe in reincarnation). The main difference between classic Hindu teaching on reincarnation and New Age reincarnation is that the Hindu believes the human soul can come back as a lower life-form, whereas the New Age spiritualist believes in upward mobilization. Marianne Williamson writes about "a karmic consequence of the lives we lived yesterday and the lives we live today."

An Ancient Belief System

We stated that New Age spirituality is syncretic. It borrows from several religions and belief systems. We have talked about some of these in previous chapters, and others are presented here for the first time. Here's a rundown:

- *Hinduism*—New Age spirituality draws heavily from the ancient religion of Hinduism (chapter 7), although it departs in one significant way. It's true that the New Age concepts of monism, pantheism, and reincarnation come from Hinduism. But whereas the true Hindu denies the world and self, New Agers affirm and glorify the self.

- *Buddhism*—As we learned in chapter 8, Buddhism teaches meditation and spiritual enlightenment (nirvana), which are key influences in New Age thought and practice. In particular, New Agers favor Zen Buddhism, which teaches that you prepare for enlightenment by clearing your conscious mind of the clutter that blocks true intuition and insight.

- *Taoism*—Taoism (chapter 9) teaches that ultimate reality is beyond categories. Opposing values (yin and yang) such as beauty and ugliness, simple and complex, and right and wrong are merely relative. There is no absolute truth— a foundational belief of New Age spirituality. Early Taoism combined meditation with breathing techniques—a popular New Age practice.

- *Gnosticism*—This ancient Greek philosophy was a system of belief that taught salvation by knowledge (*gnosis* is the Greek word for "knowledge"). According to the Gnostics, the material world was created by one of a series of lesser deities (called *aeons*) that came from the single

Intuition and Insight

Intuition and insight are a big part of contemporary New Age teaching, but you can trace the roots of these beliefs in the power of the mind to the nineteenth century, when the New Thought school and transcendentalism were taking hold. The idea behind intuition and insight is that you let go of reason and connect with the Divine Mind. The transcendentalists believed that all religions were basically true and existed to unite the conscious mind with God.

New Age author and teacher James Redfield wrote *The Celestine Prophecy,* based on ancient Peruvian manuscripts containing the nine key insights into life itself: "Insights each human being is predicted to grasp sequentially, one insight, then another, as we move toward a completely spiritual culture on Earth."

eternal principle (the big God). Gnosticism led to *dualism,* which is the idea that the eternal principle (God) and matter are the two ultimate (but separate) forces in the universe. God is the good force and matter is the evil force. The human soul is caught in the material world, but each person has a "divine spark of light" that can be released when he or she taps into the eternal spiritual energy of the universe through knowledge. Most New Age spiritualism can trace its roots to Gnosticism and dualism.

- *Native American religions*—Traditional Native American religions recognize three levels of spiritual beings: supreme god, nature spirits, and ancestor spirits. Of these, the nature spirits are held in highest regard. The world is full of living personal spirits who inhabit plants, animals, even rocks and water. The New Age belief in a sacred Earth is consistent with these traditions. Also, the common Native American practice of shamanism has been embraced by some popular New Age teachers (a *shaman* heals through contact with the spirits). Don Miguel Ruiz is a shaman (he's also a trained medical doctor) who guides individuals to personal freedom through his books *The Four Agreements* and *The Mastery of Love.*

- *Occultism and spiritism*—*Occultism* is a belief in a power based on hidden knowledge about the universe and its hidden forces. New Age spirituality focuses on this hidden knowledge. We can trace the origins of this thinking to the Theosophical Society, founded in New York in 1875 by Madame Helena Blavatsky and Henry Olcott, who taught that spiritually connected humans are led through a type of spiritual evolution through the "Ascended Masters," who are reincarnated beings. Theosophy (which means "divine wisdom") teaches that

*W*e now experience that we live not in a material universe, but in a universe of dynamic energy. Everything extant is a field of sacred energy that we can sense and intuit.

James Redfield, author of The Celestine Prophecy

God is a universal divine principle and that all religions contain a common truth.

Ron Rhodes defines *spiritism* as "the practice of attempting communication with departed human or extra-human intelligence… through the agency of a human medium." Years ago mediums were confined to gypsy trailers or circus sideshows, but today you'll find mediums on prime-time television, only these guys practice *channeling* (another name for *spiritism*). James Van Praagh has been communicating with the dead for several years now, landing his book *Talking to Heaven* on the top of the *New York Times* bestsellers list. And the psychic medium John Edward is now "Crossing Over" on his own television show. Not all New Age practitioners agree with these psychics, but they have millions of followers.

*T*wo-thirds of Americans claim to have had a psychic experience, and 40 percent believe they have personally been in contact with someone who has died.

The New Age and You

So now you know the background, the history, and the influences of New Age spirituality. What does that mean to you? Let us suggest a couple of implications. First, regardless of what you think of New Age spirituality, you have to admit that it sounds appealing. You can't write it off as a passing fad. The number of people who advocate and appreciate New Age thinking is growing exponentially because more and more people want to believe in

- a world of peace and unity rather than a world filled with hatred and conflict,

- complete integrity in all things,

- health and prosperity rather than sickness and poverty, and

- the potential of the human spirit to overcome great odds and achieve the impossible.

Second, you have to evaluate the New Age worldview on an objective level and see how it measures up to the testable Christian worldview. You can't go by what you *feel;* you have to test this belief system against the truth of God's Word.

Christianity Is an Open System

Don't ever let anyone tell you that Christianity is a closed-minded, intolerant belief system. Christianity is the only legitimate spiritual system that encourages its followers to test any belief against what God has said in His Word. An example of this occurred in the early church when the apostle Paul and his sidekick Silas were spreading the Good News message concerning the resurrection of Jesus. They went to the city of Berea, where the people weren't sure about the content of their message. The historical record in the book of Acts says that the Bereans were open-minded because "they searched the Scriptures day after day to check up on Paul and Silas, to see if they were really teaching the truth" (Acts 17:11). The result was that many skeptics—including Jews and Gentiles and men and women—believed. As Jesus once said, "And you will know the truth, and the truth will set you free" (John 8:32).

So let's test the basic message of New Age spirituality by looking at three foundational New Age beliefs. Keep in mind that there is no single set of New Age creeds or doctrines, but there are recurring principles, so let's consider the top three and then test each one against the truth of the Bible.

New Age Belief #1: God is who (or what) you want Him to be.

The god of the New Age is an impersonal force or divine principle. Everything that exists is part of God, and God is present in everything. There's no such thing as a personal supreme being. The New Age god is more of an "it" than a "He," and "it" is part of the collective consciousness. There's no such thing as a Creator God because everything that's here has always been here.

What the Bible says about God: The God of the Bible is personal, powerful, and active. He exists apart from His creation, yet He is involved in it. God created the universe at a single point in time (Genesis 1:1), and He holds it all together through Jesus (Colossians 1:17). In the New Age belief system, Jesus is merely a "way-shower" to the great consciousness (the "Christ") of the universe. Jesus declares in the Bible that He is the only way to God (John 14:6).

New Age Belief #2: Truth is what you want it to be.

New Agers believe that "truth" is revealed to individuals in different ways. The Bible has some truth, but it is hidden and therefore must be interpreted subjectively. And truth is not static. It can (and does) change as enlightened New Age spiritualists and channelers receive revelations from ancient spirit entities. Ron Rhodes writes about Kevin Ryerson, who is Shirley MacLaine's channeler. Ryerson has channeled the basic New Age "truth" that "you are God, you have unlimited potential, you create your own reality, and there is no death."

What the Bible says about truth: Truth in the Bible is rooted in reality, and we can trust it because the Bible is the Word of God, the Author of truth. The objective truths and principles of the Bible are consistent with the testable truths of the natural world, such as history, science, and philosophy. And the Bible is true when it talks about the supernatural world as well, as verified by the 100 percent accuracy rate of Bible prophecy.

New Age Belief #3: Salvation depends on you.

In her book *Dancing in the Light,* Shirley MacLaine wrote, "I *know* that I exist, therefore I AM. I know the god-source exists. Therefore, IT IS. Since I am part of that force, then I AM that I AM." That pretty much summarizes the New Age belief about humanity's need for salvation. Since you are God, you don't need to be saved. In fact, the tragedy of the human race is that you don't know you're divine. New Agers believe that many people are trapped by their misconceptions, so all they need to do is develop a new consciousness (through an expensive New Age seminar, of course) through personal transformation.

What the Bible says about salvation: The Bible is realistic and truthful about the need of humankind for salvation. All have sinned—that is, every one of us has failed to come up to God's perfect standard (Romans 3:23)—and only those who accept God's free gift of salvation through Jesus Christ will be restored to a relationship with God (Romans 5:10).

---

*T*he choice for every person confronted with New Age beliefs comes down to a choice between two realities: the alternate reality of the New Age or the reality of the Bible.

What's That Again?

1. The influence of New Age spirituality is embedded in all aspects of society: health care, business, science, politics, sports, and entertainment.

2. Many New Age practitioners are thoughtful professionals who have a common vision to transform society and bring about a new era of harmony and human progress.

3. Although there is no central authority or set of beliefs, New Age spirituality has characteristics of monism, pantheism, deification of humanity, transformation, ecological centeredness, and a belief in a new world order.

4. New Age beliefs are rooted in Hinduism, Buddhism, Taoism, gnosticism, Native American religions, and occultism and spiritism.

5. The New Age and the Bible present different realities about God, truth, and salvation.

Dig Deeper

Fritz Ridenour's *So What's the Difference?* contains information on 20 worldviews, faiths, and religions. This bestselling book has been around for nearly 25 years, but it was recently updated and expanded. The chapter on the New Age is concise and informative.

The Universe Next Door by James Sire is another classic book that's been updated to include a chapter on the New Age. Dr. Sire is an expert on the significant impact that Eastern religions and naturalism have had on current Western thinking.

Ron Rhodes is an expert on the New Age. His book *The Challenge of the Cults and New Religions* has a great chapter on the New Age. He also wrote the chapter on the New Age movement in the book *Truth and Error*.

■ ■ ■

*Q*uestions for *R*eflection and *D*iscussion

1. How can believing in "no god" be considered a religion or a faith?

2. What belief system is encompassed by the term "New Age spirituality"?

3. Can you identify some examples of New Age influences in our culture?

4. If you were making an analytical comparison, would you determine it is easier to live life as a Christian or as a New Age spiritualist? Give reasons for your answer.

5. What are the benefits and dangers of a faith system that has no central authority or set of beliefs?

6. When a New Age spiritualist speaks of "transformation," what does he or she mean? What is the Bible's concept of transformation?

7. What common ground is there for a New Age spiritualist and a Christian on the subject of the environment? How might they differ in their perspectives?

◻ ▦ ◻

Moving On . . .

Now that you've tasted the New Age onion, we hope that you are more aware of this very popular belief system. We also hope that you recognize why New Age spirituality is so tasty and attractive to tens of millions of people, many of whom are people you know. Some of them are your fellow workers, a few are your family members, and perhaps one or two are your friends at church. They are sincere, well-meaning people who are desperately seeking some kind of spiritual reality, and they think they've found it in the amalgam of beliefs called New Age spirituality.

By contrast, the people who are devoted to the belief systems in the next chapter have little, if any, interest in spiritual things. They are completely human-centered, with no room for God or anything with godlike characteristics. That's not to say that these anti-believers don't think about God. We happen to believe that they think about God a great deal because in order to deny God exists, you have to deal with His supernatural presence in our natural world.

*C*hapter 11

How can I believe in God when just
last week I got my tongue caught in
the roller of an electric typewriter?

Woody Allen

At first, you might have wondered why we are including a chapter on atheism in a book about world religions. After all, if atheists don't believe in a god, then they don't have a religion, right? Well, not so fast there, buckaroo. Just because they don't believe in God doesn't mean that they aren't religious. They have a religion. It is a religion of "no god." There are some pretty interesting ramifications from a belief in "no god," and those ramifications are the essence of the atheists' religion (although they aren't quick to admit some of them).

And, you might be thinking, what's the deal with Darwin? How does he merit getting his name in a chapter title? Well, Darwin's theories have been adopted as a belief system by many people; it is a belief system with a doctrine of "no god." Without a doubt, there is a religion of naturalism (although its adherents would never characterize their beliefs as a religion since that term smacks too much of god, of which there isn't one).

You won't find a building in your town with a sign that reads: "First Church of Atheism." And there won't be a temple dedicated to St. Darwin the Divine. But don't let that fool you. These are real religions that we'll be dealing with in this chapter.

Atheism, Darwinism, and Naturalism:
Imagine a World Without God

$\mathcal{W}$hat's $\mathcal{A}$head

- [ ] Atheism: No Reason to Believe
- [ ] Darwinism: A Reason Not to Believe
- [ ] Naturalism: An Anti-God Worldview

*I*n this chapter we leave those religions that believe in a god or gods, and we step into territory where any possibility of the existence of God is disregarded. Actually, the length of our stride takes us a lot further than that. We'll be in a place where the existence of God is not only denied, but there is also open hostility toward even the slightest suggestion of the possibility that a higher power exists. In other words, we'll be looking at a "no god" belief that has evolved into an "anti-god" belief.

Unlike other chapters, we don't have to go to the ancient past or to foreign lands to find these no-god and anti-god philosophies. They exist all around us in our contemporary culture. You will find the doctrine of these beliefs expressed throughout our society: in the media, in the educational systems (from grade school to the universities), in our legislatures, and at the local Starbucks. We may not be dealing with traditional religions, but these are nonetheless beliefs and philosophies that impact the questions of faith and destiny. Just like orthodox religions, these current cultural ideologies address questions such as, Where did I come from? What happens after I die? What is the meaning of life?

A Quick Look at Atheism and Anti-God Groups

- Atheists claim to comprise one-fifth of the world's population.

- Proponents of naturalism and neo-Darwinism predominate in the fields of academia, politics, and journalism.

- In the occult arena, estimates range from a low of 50,000 to 400,000 or more for participants in the Wiccan and witchcraft groups.

- There aren't published statistics on Satanists, but one estimate puts the number of self-professed Satanists at less than 6000 worldwide.

Atheism: No Reason to Believe

You probably think that you already know the definitions of an agnostic and an atheist. We thought we did, too, until we began the research for this book. Actually, the definitions (and the ramifications of those definitions) are a bit more complicated than it seems on the surface.

Let's go to an objective source for a working definition of some important terms. From the *Harper Collins Dictionary of Religion* we learn this:

- *Theism* is the belief in the existence of one or more divine beings. With a few exceptions, most of the religions discussed in the previous chapters would fall into this category.

- *Agnosticism* is the view that there is insufficient evidence for the existence or nonexistence of God. Agnosticism functions as an intellectual mid-position between theism and atheism. (The term was coined in 1869 during the Victorian debate over Western biblical faith and the scientific theories of Darwin.) Pure Buddhism and pure Confucianism, if such things exist, might be considered to fall in this category. Strictly speaking, they don't believe in a deity, but they are not incompatible with philosophies and religions that involve one or more deities. As is the trademark of all agnostics, they don't really take a position on God one way or the other.

- *Atheism* denies the existence of any supernatural beings. There is no form of transcendent order or meaning in the universe. According to the atheist, any notion of god is merely fiction created by humans and beyond rational thinking. In practice, atheism denotes a way of life conducted in disregard of any alleged supernatural reality.

You might be thinking, "Hey, that is exactly what I thought. The three possibilities boil down to 'God,' 'maybe God,' or 'no God.' It is as simple as that." Well, that's what we thought too. But it is not as simple as that. It turns out that there is a division within the atheist movement. They categorize themselves as being either *negative* or *positive* atheists. Here is how they further refine the definition of *atheism:*

- *A weak-position atheist:* This person believes, for himself or herself alone, that there is no god. Maybe God really exists, but they haven't been convinced of it. Other people are free to believe or disbelieve in God's existence. But for the weak-position atheists personally, they choose to believe in the nonexistence of God until they are convinced otherwise. (Sometimes this position is referred to as *negative* atheism.)

- *A strong-position atheist:* This person believes that absolutely, positively, there is no God. The strong-position atheist believes this is a universal truth. This definition became somewhat popular among atheistic writers during the twentieth century. (Sometimes this position is referred to as *positive* atheism.)

The distinction between the weak-position atheist and the strong-position atheist is an important one. It involves who carries the burden of proof.

Who's Gonna Carry the Burden of Proof? I Know! Let's Give It to the Theist!

You are already familiar with the concept of the "burden of proof." (Unless you have already had some unfortunate personal experience with the criminal justice system, just think about the O. J. Simpson trial, the Martha Stewart trial, or any television drama involving the criminal courts.) The "burden of proof" is on the prosecutor (the D.A.) to convince the jury that the defendant is guilty. If the prosecutor doesn't present enough convincing evidence, then the defendant is declared "not guilty."

It is the declared intention of atheists to put the burden of proof for the existence of God on the theists. They don't want to be put in the position of having to prove the nonexistence of God. They know it can't be done. As was stated in *Positive Atheism Magazine*, "One cannot prove a negative existential claim (that is, a claim that a thing does not exist)." For this reason, the distinction between the weak position and the strong position of atheism becomes very important. With weak-position atheism, the burden of proof falls on the theist. With strong-position atheism, however, it is the atheist that carries the burden of proof. Here is how it breaks down:

> ***The weak-position atheist says:*** "I don't believe in God because no one has provided me with any credible evidence that God exists." This position puts the theist on the defensive. The theist must present evidence to persuade the weak-position atheist.
>
> ***The strong-position atheist says:*** "Absolutely, positively, there is no god." In response to this dogmatic position, the theistic can say, "So prove it." This means that the strong-position atheist has to go on the defensive.

Atheists are well aware of this burden-of-proof issue, and they want to avoid carrying it. Consequently, they advocate using a weak-position definition of atheism even for a person who has a strong-position belief. (This is not a lie because the weak-position definition is broad enough to include proponents of the strong position.) Using a weak-position description of atheism will always put the burden of proof on the theist. This is purely and simply a debating strategy, which the atheists aren't embarrassed to admit. *Positive Atheism Magazine* suggests using weak-position terminology to avoid the burden-of-proof issue:

> With the weak definition, the strong-position atheist can participate in a lengthy debate with a theistic apologist without ever disclosing his or her wholesale dismissal of the entire god question, and without once ever being called upon to prove anything. (A careless presentation of the strong position could open itself to the Burden of Proof.) And the strong-position atheist can, through restraint, make much more of an impact on the listener. The main point here is that the theist is the one making the claim, so the theist must first describe what he or she is claiming, and secondly make a strong case for the claim. By showing that the claim itself is invalid, that it is not worthy of our attention, we don't need to deal with any counterclaims.

Atheists also recognize that the strong-position definition sounds too dogmatic and intolerant. Although many atheists espouse the strong position, the leaders of the atheism movement prefer the weak definition because the strong position does appear intolerant and because "it does sound rather untenable." They acknowledge that the most persistent objection to the strong position of atheism is that it sounds dogmatic and unscientific. Advancing the strong position in public debate forces all atheists (both strong-position and weak-position) to prove the nonexistence of God, invoking the burden of proof.

Atheists are quick to acknowledge that the strong position has disadvantages in public discussions at the popular level because it is easy to portray as dogmatic, unreasonable, and thus unscientific. To avoid public relations and marketing catastrophes, the atheism movement tries to show that the strong position of atheism, far from being the only form of atheism, is the rarest among atheistic positions. Instead, they advance the weak position of atheism. From this perspective, they shift the burden of proof to the theists. Here is how *Positive Atheism Magazine* describes the ideal sequence when a theist talks to a weak-position atheist about the existence of God:

- It must be realized that we are dealing entirely with claims—claims that various deities exist.

- In discussing such claims, it is always the person making the claim [the theist] who is responsible for providing evidence and strong argument.

- The person listening to the claim [the atheist] need not make any argument at all.

- The listener [the atheist] does not need to disprove a claim in order to reject it.

- If the person making the claim [the theist] fails to make a convincing case, the listener rightly rejects the claim as falsehood (or suspends judgment, based upon the strength of the claim). In either event, the listener ends up lacking a belief in the object of the claim.

- It is never the negative [weak-position] atheist's responsibility to prove or disprove anything. That job belongs to the person making the claim, which is the theist.

Don't get the wrong impression. The atheists believe that the strong position is defensible; they just prefer to shift the burden of proof on the theists. Atheists can articulate the nature and range of their nonbelief, and they can discuss their reasons for rejecting theism. They do so primarily by dismissing the religions of theists as being beliefs that consist entirely of controversial and untestable claims.

Darwinism: A Reason Not to Believe

Until the mid-1800s, most atheists in the Western world had to maintain a low profile. After all, anti-God sentiment was not too popular before then. (Just ask anyone who witnessed the Salem witch trials.) George H. Smith, an American philosopher of atheism and libertarianism, has acknowledged that prior to 1859, atheism was "not an intellectually tenable position." Until that time, the existence of the world, humanity, and all of nature was a compelling argument in favor of creation by God. There was simply no other credible explanation.

---

*C*hristianity, with some exceptions, has never explicitly advocated human misery; it prefers instead to speak of sacrifices in this life so that benefits may be garnered in the life to come. One invests in this life, so to speak, and collects interest in the next. Fortunately for Christianity, the dead cannot return for a refund.

George H. Smith, from Atheism: The Case Against God

But in 1859, a relatively obscure scientist by the name of Charles Darwin became fascinated with his observations from selective-breeding experiments. From these observations, he developed a most interesting hypothesis of natural selection. This hypothesis formed the basis of his book *On the Origin of Species*. Here are the basic points of Darwinism today:

> *Random mutation:* All plants and animals—any organisms that exist—are the product of the random interplay of the known processes of heredity.
>
> *Natural selection:* Differential reproduction in organisms occurs as weak traits give way to stronger ones (survival of the fittest).

This was pretty controversial stuff, but the real shocker came in Darwin's subsequent book, *The Descent of Man*, when he promoted the theory of common descent. This theory claimed that all living creatures are descended from a single ancestor. Here is what Darwin was saying in his theories:

- Life started on its own as a tiny cell that developed over time into all forms of life, including humans.

- Nature acted like a breeding machine and produced biological changes. As useful new traits appeared, they were passed on to the next generation. Harmful traits (or those of little value) were eliminated by Darwin's mechanism of natural selection.

- While these changes were small, over time and generations they accumulated until organisms developed new limbs, or organs, or other body parts. Given enough time, the organisms changed so much that they didn't resemble their ancestors anymore.

Darwin acknowledged that the fossil evidence didn't support this theory of evolution. For the theory to be correct, there would need to be innumerable transitional life-forms, but geology hadn't yet revealed evidence to prove his theories to be correct. He claimed that as the science and techniques of paleontology (fossil finding) progressed, the fossils of transitional life-forms would be found.

Micro Versus Macro

Darwin presented a theory of evolution. There are two types of evolution. *Microevolution* refers to minor variations at or below the species level. Darwin worked in this field and had scientific proof that variations can occur within a species. Based on this research, Darwin proposed a theory of *macroevolution* in which one species, over time, would evolve into a new species. He had no evidence to support the macroevolution theory.

Darwin Gave the Atheists What They Wanted (Almost)

By his theory of macroevolution, Darwin was saying that people were not created by a purposeful being (God). Instead, people are just the product of a random evolutionary process. As you might imagine, this theory was very popular with the atheists. Although it was just a theory, it gave them a sufficient basis to reject God as Creator of the universe. As Henry Osborn (head of the American Museum of Natural History and proponent of evolution) said in

1925, "From the period of the earliest stages of Greek thought, man has been eager to discover some natural cause of evolution, and to abandon the idea of super-natural intervention in the order of nature." Although it was just a theory when it was articulated, the atheists relied upon it as incontrovertible evidence against the existence of God.

Darwin's theory has survived and flourished since he proclaimed it in 1859. It is taught as a fundamental precept of biological science without any disclaimer or mention of anomalies or ambiguities. The scientific establishment adheres to the original principles (with minor revisions that are referred to as neo-Darwinism) and rejects any notion of God.

Within the last several decades, our culture has revered science. It is considered the only valid test for knowledge and truth. If it is "science," then we believe it. Anything else—things deemed *unscientific*—are dismissed. Particularly within our Western society, neither philosophy, nor religion, nor literature, nor law, nor music, nor art can make any such cognitive claim. (This is especially true of religion, which is considered to have no universal truth that is applicable to all peoples.) For most of us, these other disciplines are rejected as sources of truth in favor of science. Many people (especially those within the science community) see this as just a matter of intellectual honesty:

- Philosophy is just a bunch of people sitting around thinking lofty thoughts.

- Theology is just a matter of faith—you can believe whatever you want to believe (although you might have to disengage your brain to do it).

- Art is the appreciation of colors and shapes but has no tangible benefit.

- The law is just a bunch of rules that are complicated and arbitrarily enforced.

But science leads our culture and stands at the forefront of intellectual integrity. It has given us technology that has improved our lives. It has found cures for our diseases. It informs us about our past and gives us the ability to look into the depths of outer space.

And the findings and benefits of science are universally applicable to peoples of all countries, ethnicities, and faiths. Science seems to be the only universal constant in our lives.

There are two things which make it impossible to believe that this world is the successful work of an all-wise, all-good, and at the same time, all-powerful being; firstly the misery which abounds in it everywhere; and secondly, the obvious imperfection of its highest product, man, who is a burlesque of what he should be.

Arthur Schopenhauer, from "Studies in Pessimism:
On the Sufferings of the World"

Naturalism: An Anti-God Worldview

The legacy of Darwin is the religion of Darwinism. But that name isn't very catchy, so sociologists and philosophers refer to it as *naturalism*. Of course, it is not a religion in the traditional sense (no stained-glass windows, no rituals, and no sacred dance movements). So while few people acknowledge it as a religion, everybody considers it as a *worldview* (a way to view the world that impacts your perspective on reality).

Dr. Hazen Adds...

Bruce and Stan make a very important connection here. Because it is so difficult to define exactly what a religion is, many scholars have simply begun to look at different worldviews as religious expressions. The Darwinist and naturalist worldviews play an important religious role for many people by answering questions that have traditionally been answered by the world religions, such as, Where did I come from? What is ultimately real? Where am I going? What is life all about?

Here is how naturalists (Darwinists) view the world:

- Everything that exists is the result of natural causes. All living creatures are the result of a chance collision of atoms that, through time and random, undirected processes, have evolved to their present state.

- As humans, we are at the top of the evolutionary chain.

- With our intelligence, we can use science to harness nature for our best purposes.

- The solution to society's problems can be found within the scope of intelligence and ingenuity.

Notice that this is a worldview that excludes God. There is no need for God. There is no room for God. This "no god" worldview has significant ramifications for society:

Morality: There is no divinely imposed standard for morality (because there is no deity). Issues of morality are purely relative. We can construct our own morality, changing it to suit our time, circumstances, and personal preferences.

Multiculturalism: All cultures are morally equivalent. Each person can find his identity in his or her ancestral history, race, gender, or ethnicity. Within such parameters, cultural practices must be respected without a judgment or determination by other people as to what cultural practices may be right or wrong.

Politics and government: Human nature is essentially good, and we can create the right social and economic structures to achieve peace and prosperity. The real hope for a successful society lies within our effort and intelligence.

Ethics: There is no universal code of ethics. Human beings must create their own ethical standards according to the times and their current stage of enlightenment. We cannot look to anything beyond ourselves because there is nothing higher than ourselves (except if we happen to eventually encounter extraterrestrial alien life-forms). So the propriety of matters such as abortion, euthanasia, and cloning are to be decided by our collective wisdom.

Naturalism Is Anti-God

As can be seen from the preceding discussion, God is irrelevant in the worldview of naturalism. But naturalism goes further than just removing God from a vital role in the culture. Naturalism disregards and denigrates anyone who adheres to a theistic belief. This anti-God posture is the result of the primary implications of naturalism:

> **Implication #1: Nature is the only reality.** The particles that comprise matter and energy, along with natural laws, are the only reality. Here is how philosopher William Halverson explains it:
>
> > Naturalism asserts, first of all, that the primary constituents of reality are material entities…. I am not denying the reality—the real existence—of such things as hopes, plans, behavior, language, logical inferences, and so on. What I am asserting, however, is that anything that is real is, in the last analysis, explicable as a material entity or as a form or function or action of a material entity.
>
> **Implication #2: Nature is a closed system.** According to naturalism, the universe is a closed system. There is nothing outside of this closed system that can influence or affect it. Here is Halverson's clarification of this point:
>
> > The world is, to use a very inadequate metaphor, like a gigantic machine whose parts are so numerous and whose processes are so complex that we have thus far been able to achieve only a very partial and fragmentary understanding of how it works. In principle, however, everything that occurs is ultimately explicable in terms of the properties and relations of the particles of which matter is composed.

Naturalism's strict adherence to these two implications leads to a third:

> **Implication #3: Theists are out of touch with reality.** If someone believes in a supposed supernatural being, that person is dealing with illusion rather than reality. God is a product of an overactive (and/or guilty) imagination. Any theistic notion is the product of irrational,

unscientific thinking. Philosopher Halverson puts it this way:

> Theism says, "In the beginning, God"; naturalism says, "in the beginning, matter." If the theoretical goal of science—an absolutely exhaustive knowledge of the natural world—were to be achieved, there would remain no reality of any other kind about which we might still be ignorant. The "ultimate realities," according to naturalism, are not the alleged objects of the inquiries of theologians; they are the entities that are the objects of investigations by chemists, physicists, and other scientists. To put the matter very simply: materialism is true.

If God is an irrational concept, then anyone who is a theist is an imbecile. Two examples should suffice to illustrate the hostility of the adherents of naturalism against theists:

- When U.S. Supreme Court Justice Antonin Scalia announced in a speech that he believed in miracles and in the resurrection of Jesus Christ, he was belittled and criticized in all segments of society. *Washington Post* columnist Richard Cohen stated that Scalia should be disqualified from handling any cases involving church-state issues (thereby implying that only atheists should be allowed to decide such issues).

- One of the leading proponents of the worldview of naturalism is Oxford scientist and author Richard Dawkins. He cannot tolerate theistic beliefs and has made his opinion well-known: "It is absolutely safe to say that if you meet somebody who claims not to believe in evolution, that person is ignorant, stupid or insane (or wicked, but I'd rather not consider that)."

But Naturalism Has a Wedgie

The worldview of naturalism flourished during the last half of the twentieth century. However, within the last decade or so, a group of top-notch scientists from different specialties have burst into the science lab to promote scientific research referred to as "intelligent design." All of a sudden, the arguments for a supernatural power beyond our own universe have come out of the theology/philosophy closet and are bubbling like a test tube held over a Bunsen burner. (Please excuse our mix of metaphors.)

> $\mathcal{G}$od, equally with gods, angels, demons, spirits, and other small spiritual fry, is a human product, arising inevitably from a certain kind of ignorance and a certain degree of helplessness with respect to man's external environment.
>
> *Julian Huxley*

The intelligent-design movement is driving a wedge into the closed thinking of naturalism. Intelligent-design theory examines the order and complexity of scientific evidence with the conclusion that random chance could not be the cause. These scientists have established that there exist well-defined methods that, on the basis of observational features of the world, are capable of reliably distinguishing intelligent cause from undirected natural causes. One of the leading proponents of intelligent design is Dr. William Dembski. Here is how he describes the role of intelligent-design theory:

> From observable features of the natural world, intelligent design infers to an *intelligence* responsible for those features. The world contains events, objects and structures that exhaust the explanatory resources of undirected natural causes and that can be adequately explained only by recourse to intelligent causes.

The intelligent-design movement is rattling the cage of those who adhere to the worldview of naturalism because this debate is taking place in the "sacred" realm of science. It is important to note that the scientists supporting intelligent design do not oppose Darwinism because it contradicts the Bible or challenges sacred notions of Christianity. For these scientists, it is not about religion

The Beliefs of Atheism

What About...	According to Atheism...
God	Who? What? Don't waste my time.
Humanity	Humans are part of the random evolutionary development of nature. We were not created. We just happened. Except for our status atop the evolutionary chain, there is no particular significance to our existence. We are capable of solving the problems of society with our intelligence.
Sin	The word *sin* connotes some activity that is prohibited by God. There is no God, so there is no such thing as sin. That doesn't mean that all conduct is good. Murder is obviously bad, but there are no "eternal consequences" attached to it.
Salvation and the Afterlife	There is no afterlife. You live, you die, that's it. There is nothing to be saved from, so *salvation* is a nonsensical word.
Morals	Everything is relative and personal. There is no absolute standard of right and wrong. It is whatever an individual wants to do, or whatever standard a society collectively agrees to impose. Unfortunately, too many people are trying to impose an outdated and archaic morality based on the fables of the Bible. There is nothing sacred, or even necessarily correct, about the Bible's standard of morality.
Worship	There is nothing supernatural god-wise for us to worship. The things that are worthy of worship are humanity's achievements, particularly in the areas of science and technology.
Jesus	There is no single opinion about Jesus, except that He wasn't God because there is no God. He claimed to be something that doesn't exist (God). At worst, that made Him a fake and a fraud. At best, He was just mentally deluded, in which case He was just a fruitcake.

(some of them describe themselves as agnostics); it is about the integrity of scientific investigation.

The intelligent-design scientists do not think that Darwin was totally out to lunch. They acknowledge that Darwin's mutation-selection mechanism constitutes a respectable concept in biology that merits continued investigation. But they challenge Darwinism's all-encompassing claim that this undirected mechanism accounts for all the diversity of life and the common descent of all life-forms.

Most Darwinists aren't very friendly toward the intelligent-design movement. The "no god" concept is threatened with the continuing research that points, scientifically, to an intelligent designer. Whether the research is through the telescope or the microscope, the weight of new scientific evidence is falling on the side of intelligent design. This weakens the position of naturalism since the theist can no longer be ignored. In the worldview where science is revered, the theist can now enter the discussion with empirical data. The "closed universe" of naturalism is being cracked open by the wedge of intelligent design.

What's That Again?

1. Atheism denies the existence of any superhuman being. According to the atheist, any notion of God is merely fiction created by humans that is beyond rational thinking.

2. A weak-position atheist believes that there is no God as far as he or she is concerned, but respects the right of other people to believe in God's existence. In fact, the weak position acknowledges that God may actually exist (but enough proof hasn't been provided to persuade the atheist yet). The strong-position atheist, on the other hand, claims that the non-existence of God is a universal truth.

3. Atheists prefer to use a weak-position definition in public in an attempt to shift the burden of proving God's existence on the theist.

4. Darwin's theory of macroevolution (all species of life evolving from a single organism) gave the atheists a basis on which to explain the existence of the universe without it being God-caused.

5. Naturalism is the worldview that excludes God. It contends that reality is limited to material elements and nature. Scientific investigation is the basis on which everything should be evaluated. Matters such as morality and ethics are relative because there is no absolute standard imposed upon humanity. Theists are dismissed from public discourse because they are not dealing with reality.

6. A fast-growing branch of scientific research involves intelligent design. The order of the universe and the complexity of matter within it point to an intelligent designer rather than random chance and mutation. The intelligent-design movement gives the theist scientific credibility and presents a significant challenge to the worldview of naturalism.

Dig Deeper

We have several books to recommend that give an excellent presentation of the naturalism/Darwinism philosophy, along with a rational counterargument.

Faith and Reason: Searching for a Rational Faith by Ronald H. Nash was designed to serve as a college textbook for courses dealing with contemporary philosophical trends, but the writing style isn't hyper-technical (which means it was simple enough that even we could understand it).

Phillip E. Johnson is a law professor at University of California at Berkeley. He is internationally known for his debates against Darwinists on the issue of whether the world came into existence by chance (the Darwin view) or by the work of an intelligent designer (God). In other words, Johnson is an expert in the whole "god versus no god" controversy. Although he has written many books, the one that relates best to this chapter is his *Reason in the Balance: The Case Against Naturalism in Science, Law and Education*.

If you are an atheist (or agnostic) looking for evidence about the existence of God, or if you are a Christian in search of facts that support the reliability of the Bible and the claims of Christ, read *The Best of Josh McDowell: A Ready Defense*. Josh has spoken to over ten million people about the credibility of the evidence in support of Christianity.

Charles Colson, a former henchman for President Nixon, has turned a bit philosophical (as frequently happens to prison inmates). He has coauthored *How Now Shall We Live?* with Nancy Pearcey. This book deals with the concept of establishing your personal worldview as the means for understanding reality and culture.

May we also shamelessly plug one of our own books? What's to stop us, right? In *Creation and Evolution 101* we discuss the naturalism/Darwinism viewpoint as it relates to the issues concerning the origins of the universe.

$\mathcal{Q}$uestions for $\mathcal{R}$eflection and $\mathcal{D}$iscussion

1. Explain the difference between theism, agnosticism, and atheism.

2. How do atheists avoid the burden-of-proof issue when it comes to God? Give two reasons why they do this.

3. In what ways did Darwin legitimize atheism? What parts of Darwin's theory are most compatible with atheism?

4. Explain why our culture has embraced science as the standard for truth.

5. List the basic points of the worldview known as naturalism. How do these points position naturalism against God?

6. Explain how the intelligent-design movement is creating problems for naturalism.

7. What ultimately happens to a society that embraces relativism wholeheartedly?

■ ■ ■

Moving On...

Well, we've come a long way together, haven't we? Our journey started in the deserts of the Middle East where Judaism, Christianity, and Islam began. And from the lands of the Orient and Southeast Asia, we have sojourned together through the centuries as we examined Hinduism, Buddhism, and the Eastern philosophies. That's a lot of time and ground to cover in just 250 pages. (No wonder we have calluses on our craniums.)

As we moved through time and geography, we were introduced to the major religions and their variations, combinations, and deviations. And now, here we are today, with a veritable buffet of beliefs, ranging from monotheistic religions to those of the polytheistic variety, with a smattering of no-god or even anti-god religions on the side. No one can say that he or she doesn't have enough to choose from.

Our job with this book was to present you with an overview of the major religions and spiritual beliefs. We are finished with our job. Your job, however, is not quite over. You see, there have always been three aspects to *your* part in this book:

- First, it was your responsibility to review what we wrote.

- Secondly (and this is what we shrewdly omitted at the beginning), your job also includes the responsibility of *deciding* what you believe.

- Thirdly, which we also conveniently forgot to mention, you have to *do something* with what you believe.

Please don't be upset with us for springing these responsibilities upon you at the end of the book. If you are honest with yourself, you'll admit that you knew you had these responsibilities all along. Maybe that is why you are reading this book in the first place.

And just to show you that we still have your best interests at heart, we aren't going to abandon you at this very point where our job ends and your final responsibilities begin. No, we are much too good of friends with you to leave you hanging now. That's why we have added the last part of the book—to help you in the process of deciding what to do with what you believe.

Part V
Practicing Your
Religion

Chapter 12

You have been worshiping him
without knowing who he is, and now
I wish to tell you about him.

Paul the apostle

Way back at the beginning of this book we stated that we are fully devoted followers of Jesus Christ. We tried not to let our bias as biblical Christians come through too much as we described and analyzed the world's major cults and religions. But if we did, it was only because we believe the truths of Christianity are completely—and not just partially—true.

We also told you that we are not trying to convert, cajole, or coax you into Christianity. You need to make your own choice. Now, having said that, we are going to make a bold assumption. We figure that if you've read this far, you may agree with us that the God of the Bible is the one true God, and Christianity is the one true belief system. If our assumption is correct, then continue reading this last chapter, because we're going to put your belief into a practical perspective. If our assumption is incorrect, and you're still not sure what to believe, go ahead and finish the book anyway. If nothing else, you're going to discover that there's more to Christianity than belief.

What Do You Do with What You Believe?

What's Ahead

- ▨ Know What You Believe
- ▨ Know What Others Believe
- ▨ Reach Out in Love
- ▨ Be Ready to Explain What You Believe

*T*he city of Athens in first-century Greece was a lot like a typical twenty-first century major metropolitan capital. Like present-day Paris, Athens was a cultural city with magnificent buildings and artwork of breathtaking beauty. Like New York City, Athens was the world's most famous intellectual center. Even young men from Rome went to Athens for university training. Athens was also a religious place. Scattered throughout the city, among the world-class artwork and temples, were dozens and dozens of idols, many representing the classic Greek gods.

Into this cultural and intellectual center stepped the apostle Paul, the greatest Christian missionary of all time. Aside from Jesus, Paul is considered the most influential person in the history of Christianity. The time was approximately A.D. 50, and Paul was in the middle of his second missionary journey. He was in Athens not to preach but to wait for the rest of his team to join him. Paul was probably relaxing, taking in the sights, and eating some Greek food. He wasn't looking for a debate, but he was ready to let God use him.

We want to use the story of what happened to Paul in Athens as an example of what it takes and what it means to put your beliefs into practice in a culture that includes all kinds of opposing religious and spiritual beliefs. Even though this true story happened nearly 2000 years ago, it is just as relevant as anything you could experience today.

As we walk you through this, you're welcome to follow along by reading Acts 17:16-34. You might even want to take some notes (you can write in the book—we won't mind) because this is what you need to do with what you believe.

Know What You Believe

The whole purpose of this book is to encourage you to get to know the beliefs of other people, and that's exactly what we've been doing. However, we have a warning for you (great—we wait until now to give it), and here it is:

> **You need to know your own beliefs**
> **before you study the beliefs of other people.**

Many Christians make the mistake of looking for truth in other religions and spiritual beliefs before they thoroughly know their own. When you don't start with a "plumb line" of truth to keep you focused on what's right, it's easy to get trapped in the "all roads lead to God" mentality. And what is the plumb line of truth? The Word of God. It's the only thing that will keep you straight.

It doesn't matter how smart you were before you became a Christian. The truths of God are different than the truths of the world, and the only way you can learn the truths of God is to be guided by the Holy Spirit as you consistently study the Scriptures (John 14:17).

The apostle Paul was a brilliant man. He had the equivalent of two doctorates and knew several languages. His dramatic conversion from a persecutor of Christians to a Christ-follower happened in a flash (Acts 9:1-6), yet he didn't immediately go out on the converted-Christian-celebrity speaking circuit (after getting an agent, of course). Historians tell us that Paul studied for 13 years before beginning his public preaching, teaching, and writing ministry. For three of those years he lived in the Arabian Desert.

It Happens in the Desert

There's something about the desert that inspires spiritual growth. Moses, the great deliverer of the Jews, spent 40 years in the Sinai desert before he was ready to lead God's people into the Promised Land. Even Jesus had a desert experience. Following His baptism, Jesus spent 40 days in the wilderness fasting and praying in preparation for His public ministry. What's the message for us in all of this desert stuff? We need to be in the public square, but we can't always stay there. We need a regular time to recharge our spiritual batteries by praying and reading God's Word. You may not have to go to the desert to make this happen (although an occasional spiritual retreat is a good idea), but you do need those private times with God on a daily basis in order to stay spiritually healthy.

By the time Paul got to Athens, he thoroughly knew what he believed. Now we're not suggesting that you spend 13 years studying your beliefs before learning the beliefs of other people (unless you're planning to be the greatest missionary since the apostle Paul), but you do need to study God's Word until you can confidently articulate what you know to someone who doesn't—and then continue studying for the rest of your life. There's no magic formula, but here are some basics we would suggest in your lifetime of study:

- Study the Bible systematically on your own every day.

- Regularly attend a church where the Bible is taught.

- Participate in a small group Bible study with other Christians.

- Build a library of books about the Bible and the Christian life.

- Take some college- or seminary-level Bible courses, if possible.

If that seems like a lot of work, it should! Studying the Word of God shouldn't be a breeze. It should be a *joy* and it should never be a burden, but you should never take it lightly. Here's what Paul wrote to his protégé, Timothy:

> *Work hard so God can approve you. Be a good worker, one who does not need to be ashamed and who correctly explains the word of truth* (2 Timothy 2:15).

Know What Others Believe

To illustrate why it's important to know the beliefs of other people, let's go back to the story of Paul in Athens. As he was walking around the city, he noticed all of the idols, and it troubled him (Acts 17:16). But instead of going back to his motel to get away from the spiritual darkness, Paul went into the "public square," where he talked to everyone. The Bible says he had a debate "with some of the Epicurean and Stoic philosophers" (17:18). This is where it gets interesting (and very practical).

The Epicureans and Stoics were the two major philosophy groups in Greece at that time. Here's what they believed:

- The **Epicureans,** if they believed in the gods at all, thought they existed but had no interest in people or their affairs. The chief end of life was pleasure, which they pursued through a happy and tranquil life free from pain, especially death. Because they lived as if God didn't exist, the Epicureans could be considered *atheistic materialists.*

- The **Stoics** believed that God was the world's soul who lived in all things, and that the happy life was lived as one with nature. For all practical purposes, the Stoics were *pantheistic monists.*

See what we mean? There's nothing new. These belief systems haven't changed much, and they're still with us today. In Paul's day, both of these groups were hostile to the Good News of the gospel, which is all about the resurrection of Jesus Christ. When Paul told them about Jesus, they thought he was strange. "He's pushing some foreign religion," they said (17:18). God-in-the-flesh puzzled these philosophers. They couldn't relate to Him.

So Paul, who knew their belief systems (probably better than they did), changed his tactic. He wasn't ashamed of Jesus. He was just being wise in his approach. When the philosophers asked him to further explain his beliefs, Paul didn't condemn them for their religiosity—he commended them. And he commented specifically on the inscription he had seen on one particular idol: "To an Unknown God."

Paul knew that the Athenians wanted to cover all the bases with all the gods, so they built this idol. He complimented them for their desire to know God, and then he offered to tell them about the one true God. It was a brilliant move on Paul's part, and he pulled it off because he knew what the philosophers believed.

Gerald McDermott is critical of Christians who approach people of other faiths "with the assumption that their religions are totally false or wholly demonic, and that if they accept Christ they must discard everything they have ever known about the divine." When we assume that people who hold other beliefs are completely in the dark, we risk alienating them from wanting to know more about our faith. Paul didn't do this.

Why Should We Learn Truth from Other Religions?

In his book *Can Evangelicals Learn from World Religions?* Gerald McDermott gives four reasons why we should learn about other belief systems:

1. If we are more sensitive to what other people believe, we'll be more effective.
2. Learning about other belief systems will help us appreciate our own faith more.
3. Learning from other religions will give us compassion for other people.
4. Knowing what other people believe will show us that "God is at work in more ways and lands and people than many of us had imagined."

Reach Out in Love

Even though Paul was in a hostile environment (and clearly outnumbered), he didn't get rattled. Even though the Greek philosophers thought he was babbling like a fool about that resurrection business, Paul didn't take it personally, and he didn't get defensive. He understood why they couldn't grasp the message. Later, in a letter to the Corinthian church, Paul explained that Christians shouldn't be surprised when other people don't think the Good News of the gospel makes sense. In a clear reference to his experience in Athens, Paul wrote this about God's way of working:

> *And it is foolish to the Greeks because they believe only what agrees with their own wisdom* (1 Corinthians 1:22).

It isn't foolish to them because God's plan to save people through Christ is dumb. The problem is that their minds can't grasp the things of God. They aren't on God's frequency. Paul elaborated further:

> *But people who aren't Christians can't understand these truths from God's Spirit. It all sounds foolish to them because only those who have the Spirit can understand what the Spirit means. We who have the Spirit understand these things, but others can't understand us at all* (1 Corinthians 2:14-15).

Rather than be upset with people who don't believe as we do, we need to have compassion for them. We need to reach out to them in love, realizing that without Christ, they will be eternally separated from the true God who loves them and has provided a way out of their spiritual condemnation. McDermott refers to something the great American preacher Jonathan Edwards said: "It is the loving thing to tell a man on the second floor that the first floor is on fire."

To ignore the fact that people without Christ are in trouble is heartless. McDermott writes: "Out of love for our non-Christian friends who already know something of God, we will want to share with them *more* truth, as the Spirit leads and at the proper time."

Build a Relationship

That phrase "at the proper time" is key. Alan Gomes and Kevin Lewis, two professors of theology and experts in world religions and cults, recommend that Christians build relationships with people of other religions before trying to talk them out of their beliefs. "Very few conversions happen on the doorstep," they write. Their experience shows that "most cult members convert to Christianity through Christians they have developed relationships with." Rodney Stark, a professor of comparative religions at the University of Washington, has been studying the rise in new religions. He agrees that most people aren't attracted to a particular belief system because of its doctrine. "What happens is that people form relationships and only then come to embrace a religion."

Paul wasn't in Athens long enough to build a long-term relationship with the philosophers and skeptics, but neither did he blow in and out of town. The Bible indicates that he was there for several days and was introduced to a lot of people. His sightseeing definitely took a backseat to his relationship-building. He must have earned their trust because even though they thought he was speaking foolishness, the philosophers said, "You are saying some rather startling things, and we want to know what it's all about" (Acts 17:20).

Be Ready to Explain What You Believe

That's exactly what's going to happen to you. When you build relationships in love with other people and you show respect for their beliefs, they are going to eventually ask about your faith, and you need to be ready to answer them with clarity of thought and a loving heart. The apostle Peter wrote a letter to the Christians who were experiencing opposition to their faith:

> And if you are asked about your Christian hope, always
> be ready to explain it. But you must do this in a gentle
> and respectful way (1 Peter 3:15).

This is what Paul did when the Greek philosophers asked him to explain this "new" religion. In a very reasonable yet loving way,

Paul told them about the "unknown God" who was closer to them than they realized. Here's what he said about God:

- **God is the Creator (17:24).** Paul goes back to the beginning and explains that the universe didn't come about on its own, and it hasn't always existed. God is the self-existent Creator of everything, and He is Lord over all.

- **God doesn't live in man-made temples (17:24).** An idol is merely a man-made artifact, not a representation of God. Even a temple can't contain almighty God. We may go to church to worship God, but He is not confined to our buildings.

- **God doesn't need anything from us, but we need everything from Him (17:25).** God is the Source of all life, and as such He doesn't need anything. God exists apart from all that He has made, but He gives life and breath to everything.

- **God is involved with His creation (17:26).** Nothing happens in heaven and on earth that God doesn't know about. Furthermore, He directs the affairs of people and nations.

- **God wants us to seek Him (17:27).** The reason God is so intimately involved with His created beings is that He wants a relationship with them. God may be transcendent in that He exists apart from His creation, but He is also the God who is near—so near that He isn't very far away from any of us.

- **God has given us evidence of His existence (17:28).** The reason we know God is near is that we can see the evidence of His existence and His personal involvement through creation, through His Word, and through His Son.

- **God asks everyone to turn to Him (17:29-30).** God is not sitting idly by while people worship their idols. God wants—no, He commands—that people turn away from their idolatry and turn to Him.

- *God is being patient, but someday there will be judgment (17:31).* The idea that God will eventually save everyone is wrong. God doesn't want anyone to die apart from Him, but He has set a day to bring everything to a conclusion. This will happen when Jesus returns to earth to judge the world, and God proved this by raising Jesus from the dead.

It Helps to Know the Culture

R.C. Sproul points out that when Paul talked about God as being the one in whom "we live and move and exist" (17:28), he was quoting the Greek poet Epimenides, who wrote that in Zeus "we live and are moved, and have our being." Paul then quoted the poet Aratus, who declared, "We have all to do with Zeus, for we are truly his offspring." Paul knew the Greek culture so well that he could quote their own poets. More than that, he showed the Athenians that their concept of Zeus, their number one god, was similar to the concept of the one true God. That's what Paul meant when he said to them, "You have been worshiping him without knowing who he is" (17:23).

Not Everyone Will Respond—but Some Will

You would think that after Paul's eloquent, loving, and persuasive explanation of his Christian hope, the people would have lined up to receive Christ. But that didn't happen. There were a variety of responses:

> When they heard Paul speak of the resurrection of a person who had been dead, some laughed, but others said, "We want to hear more about this later." That ended Paul's discussion with them (17:32-33).

This is what's great about the Bible. It's realistic about life and the way things are. The writer of Acts didn't have to reveal that some people laughed at Paul, but he left it in as an encouragement to the rest of us. Not everyone is going to respond to our explanations of the Christian message. Some people will even laugh. But others will want to hear more about our belief system. Notice that Paul was content to stop talking. He didn't feel the need to continue explaining or pleading with these people. He trusted God that there would be another time and another place to continue the discussion.

That's the way we need to be when we witness for Christ. The timing isn't up to us. Only God knows when and where someone will respond to His love and His plan. If some people do become believers (and some people who were listening to Paul did—see 17:34), it's because of the Holy Spirit moving in their lives, not because we were so persuasive.

Sharing Your Faith Is Not Optional

Our only responsibility is to share the hope we have because of Jesus Christ. And make no mistake, it is a responsibility. Jesus Himself gave us the command:

> Go into all the world and preach the Good News to everyone, everywhere (Mark 16:15).

The good news about the Good News is that God has brought people everywhere to your doorstep. If you had been born a generation earlier, you would have had to travel to India or China or Africa to share your faith with people who have other beliefs. But you live in a time and in a place where people with other beliefs are in your hometown, living next door to you, working alongside you, going to class with you. It doesn't matter how much truth we think they have or don't have. It's not enough just to have a belief in the one true God and the one true belief system. God's Word commands us to share the message of Jesus with those who don't know it. That's what you need to do with what you believe.

> And remember, it is a message to obey, not just to listen to. If you don't obey, you are only fooling yourself. For if you just listen and don't obey, it is like looking at your face in a mirror but doing nothing to improve your appearance. You see yourself, walk away, and forget what you look like.

*But if you keep looking steadily into God's perfect law—
the law that sets you free—and if you do what it says and
don't forget what you heard, then God will bless you for
doing it* (James 1:22-25).

What's That Again?

1. The ancient Greek city of Athens was much like our cities today: full of culture, knowledge, and religion, but lacking true belief.

2. The apostle Paul had an experience in Athens that serves as a model for what we should do with what we believe.

3. You need to know your own beliefs before you learn the beliefs of other people. This requires personal, systematic Bible study and personal involvement with other believers who do the same.

4. When you learn about other religions, you will appreciate your own faith more, and you will become more sensitive and compassionate to other people. Knowing about other spiritual beliefs also shows you that God is at work around the world.

5. The best way to convince people that they need Jesus is to first build a relationship with them.

6. When you build relationships with people, they will inevitably ask about your beliefs. You need to be ready to explain your Christian hope.

7. You are not responsible for the response of people to the gospel, but you are responsible to share your faith.

Dig Deeper

You would think that we would have run out of books by now, but we've got some more great resources to recommend.

Can Evangelicals Learn from World Religions? by Gerald R. McDermott is an interesting and useful book that will help you understand that other belief systems are closer to the truth than you might think.

Ravi Zacharias is a true world Christian. He was raised in the Hindu tradition, and he was trained in the finest schools of philosophy, but he is a brilliant Christian apologist. His book *Jesus Among Other Gods* shows you how to relate Jesus to people of other faiths and cultures.

We found a very insightful article in the February 2002 issue of *The Atlantic* called "Oh, Gods!" Journalist Toby Lester reports on the explosion of New Religious Movements (NRMs) in the twenty-first century. It's an eye-opener.

▨ ▨ ▨

*Q*uestions for *R*eflection and *D*iscussion

1. Is it important for you to come to some decision about spiritual matters and which, if any, religious faith is true? Why or why not?

2. Without using the description or label of any "brand name" faith, describe what you believe about spiritual matters.

3. What is your opinion about God, sin, humanity, Jesus, salvation, and the afterlife?

4. Is it important for you to know what other people believe? Why or why not?

5. If you are in a discussion with someone of a different faith, is it more effective to begin with identifying what you believe in common or to focus on your differences?

6. Christianity is egalitarian (which means that it is open to all people). How come people of other faiths criticize Christians as being intolerant and exclusive?

7. Describe a time when someone tried to force you to believe his or her religious views. Did you learn anything from this experience that guides how you share your faith with others?

■ ■ ■

Moving On...

We've reached the last part of our journey together through the exciting and sometimes exotic world of cults, religions, and spiritual beliefs. We've done our best to guide you through the maze, and we hope we have encouraged you to think things through—starting with your own beliefs. You may not know everything there is to know about every religion (and you never will), but at least you have a better understanding of what you believe and why it matters.

And we hope that we have encouraged you to share your faith with other people who don't know the whole truth about God. May you go out with God's wisdom and strength in the power and the name of Jesus, and may God bless you for doing it.

*A*dditional *R*esources

Space did not allow us to cover every aspect of every cult, religion, and spiritual belief. That's why we encouraged you to "Dig Deeper" at the end of every chapter. In addition to these resources, here are some key reference books and websites that provide a wealth of information:

Reference Books

Understanding the Times by David A. Noebel is a comprehensive guide to understanding the ideas and forces shaping our culture. In a mere 900 pages, Noebel thoroughly deals with the major worldviews as they relate to theology, philosophy, ethics, biology, psychology, sociology, law, politics, economics, and history.

The *World Christian Encyclopedia,* edited by David B. Barrett, is considered the only reference work in existence that analyzes the current religious fabric of the entire world (and it only takes two volumes of 800 pages each to accomplish the task).

Websites

The largest and most successful multifaith Internet website is www.beliefnet.com. Here you'll find facts, articles, and discussion forums on every major belief.

The largest network of Christian ministries can be found at www.gospelcom.net. There is a very useful index and hundreds of links.

For more information on cults and witnessing to cult members, Dr. Hazen recommends these organizations and their websites:

- Watchman Fellowship: www.watchman.org
- Alpha Omega Ministries: www.aomin.org
- Institute for Religious Research: www.irr.org
- Apologetics Index: www.apologeticsindex.org

Of course, you can always check out our website at www.christianity101online.com or e-mail us directly at info@christianity101online.com.

Index